Electronic Portfolios

CHANDOS SERIES

If you would like a full listing of current and forthcoming titles, please visit our website www.chandospublishing.com or email info@chandospublishing.com or telephone +44 (0) 1223 891358.

New authors: we are always pleased to receive ideas for new titles; if you would like to write a book for Chandos, please contact Dr Glyn Jones on email gjones@chandospublishing.com or telephone number +44 (0) 1993 848726.

Bulk orders: some organisations buy a number of copies of our books. If you are interested in doing this, we would be pleased to discuss a discount. Please email info@chandospublishing.com or telephone +44 (0) 1223 891358.

Electronic Portfolios

Personal information, personal development and personal values

SIMON GRANT

Chandos Publishing
Oxford • Cambridge • New Delhi

Chandos Publishing
TBAC Business Centre
Avenue 4
Station Lane
Witney
Oxford OX28 4BN
UK
Tel: +44 (0) 1993 848726
Email: info@chandospublishing.com
www.chandospublishing.com

Chandos Publishing is an imprint of Woodhead Publishing Limited

Woodhead Publishing Limited
Abington Hall
Granta Park
Great Abington
Cambridge CB21 6AH
UK
www.woodheadpublishing.com

First published in 2009

ISBN:
978 1 84334 401 8

© A. Simon Grant, 2009

British Library Cataloguing-in-Publication Data.
A catalogue record for this book is available from the British Library.

All rights reserved. No part of this publication may be reproduced, stored in or introduced into a retrieval system, or transmitted, in any form, or by any means (electronic, mechanical, photocopying, recording or otherwise) without the prior written permission of the Publishers. This publication may not be lent, resold, hired out or otherwise disposed of by way of trade in any form of binding or cover other than that in which it is published without the prior consent of the Publishers. Any person who does any unauthorised act in relation to this publication may be liable to criminal prosecution and civil claims for damages.

The Publishers make no representation, express or implied, with regard to the accuracy of the information contained in this publication and cannot accept any legal responsibility or liability for any errors or omissions.

The material contained in this publication constitutes general guidelines only and does not represent to be advice on any particular matter. No reader or purchaser should act on the basis of material contained in this publication without first taking professional advice appropriate to their particular circumstances. Any screenshots in this publication are the copyright of the website owner(s), unless indicated otherwise.

Typeset by Domex e-Data Pvt. Ltd.
Printed in the UK and USA.

Printed in the UK by 4edge Limited - www.4edge.co.uk

Contents

About the author		xiii
Acknowledgments		xv
Preface		xvii
1	**Introduction**	**1**
	Guide for readers	1
	E-portfolio systems: purpose, information, functionality	3
	What this book is not	4
	What is so personal?	5
	References and further reading	6
Part 1: Principles of e-portfolio systems		**7**
2	**Some scenarios of e-portfolio use**	**9**
	Assessment	9
	Presentation for transition	10
	Development of skills in general	11
	Learning to learn and reflect	12
	Application for a job	13
	References and further reading	14
3	**Who wants personal information?**	**15**
	Ourselves	16
	Educators	17
	Employers	18
	Public agencies	19

	Friends and the peer group	20
	References and further reading	21
4	**The rationale behind recording and storing personal information**	**23**
	Allowing others access to our information	23
	Reuse across time and context	24
	Coordinating permissions	24
	Recording helps self-knowledge	25
5	**Portfolio purposes outlined**	**27**
	Reflective purposes	28
	Purposes focusing on information use by others	29
	Purposes spanning use by ourselves and others	30
	Ancillary or related purposes	33
	References and further reading	37
6	**Portfolio information**	**39**
	Historical and current practice	39
	Information relevant to purposes	41
	The inherent nature of portfolio information	43
	Kinds of information that are relevant to e-portfolios	47
	One particular relationship: evidence	54
	Other aspects of portfolio information	54
	References and further reading	55
7	**Issues with portfolio information**	**57**
	Data protection outline	57
	Authentication and verification	58
	Information interoperability	60
	Centralised and distributed storage of personal information	63
	References and further reading	65

Contents

8	The need for common terms in portfolio information	67
	The positive and negative role of ICT for common terms and definitions	71
	References and further reading	73
9	**Portfolio functionality**	**75**
	Input and storage functions	76
	Management, maintenance and elaboration functions	78
	Reuse and communication functions	81
10	**Applying e-portfolio principles**	**83**
	What is the purpose?	83
	What information is relevant?	85
	What functionality is helpful?	87
	Tools for education	88
	Summary	89
	References and further reading	89
Part 2: How to do things with e-portfolio and related tools		**91**
	Introduction to this part	91
	How to choose an e-portfolio system	92
	Commercial or free/open source?	93
11	**How to use tools for assessment**	**95**
	Perspectives	97
	Why do you want to do this?	97
	Questions to think about	98
	Choice of tools	101
	Other action points to consider	102
	Summary of relevant principles	103
	References and further reading	103
12	**How to use tools for recording significant personal information**	**105**
	Perspectives	105

	Why do you want to do this?	106
	Questions to think about	108
	Choice of tools	109
	Other action points to consider	110
	Summary of relevant principles	110
	References and further reading	110
13	**How to use tools for self-presentation**	**111**
	Perspectives	111
	Why do you want to do this?	112
	Questions to think about	113
	Choice of tools	114
	Other action points to consider	116
	Summary of relevant principles	117
	References and further reading	117
14	**How to use tools provided for your own development**	**119**
	Perspectives	120
	Why do you want to do this?	120
	Questions to think about	121
	Action points to consider	124
	Choice of tools	125
	Summary of relevant principles	125
	References and further reading	125
15	**How to motivate and help others to use tools**	**127**
	General considerations on motivation	127
	Perspectives	128
	Why do you want to do this?	129
	Questions to think about	130
	Action points to consider	131
	Choice of tools	132

	Summary of relevant principles	133
	References and further reading	133
16	**How to develop e-portfolio tools**	**135**
	Perspectives	135
	Why do you want to do this?	135
	Questions to think about	136
	Action points to consider	140
	Summary of relevant principles	142
	References and further reading	142
17	**How to coordinate e-portfolio and administrative tools**	**143**
	Perspective	144
	Why do you want to do this?	144
	Questions to think about	145
	Action points to consider	146
	Choice of tools	146
	Summary of relevant principles	147
	References and further reading	147
18	**How to develop interoperability in tools**	**149**
	Perspective	150
	Why do you want to do this?	151
	Questions to think about	151
	Action points to consider	152
	Other points	156
	Summary of relevant principles	156
19	**How to publish terms for common use by tools**	**157**
	Perspective	158
	Why do you want to do this?	158
	Questions to think about	159
	Action points to consider	161

	Summary of relevant principles	163
	References and further reading	163
Part 3: Future vision		**165**
20	**Notes on portfolio environments and values**	**167**
	The possible social environments of assessment and presentation	167
	What are personal values?	172
	So why are people not (yet) more enthusiastic about e-portfolios?	173
	References and further reading	174
21	**Matching information for people**	**175**
	The difficulties of the current employment and education markets	175
	How matching should work for education and employment	176
	Development for matching	178
	Synergy with matching for other reasons	180
	References and further reading	182
22	**Personal values, identity and personality**	**183**
	Different situations and contexts	185
	Roles	187
	Different values in different contexts	188
	References and further reading	189
23	**Developing personality and personal values**	**191**
	How personal values may develop naturally	191
	Tools and practice supporting the development of values	195
	References and further reading	202
24	**Ethical development and values in society**	**203**
	Values tourism	203
	The small group	205
	Values and trust	206

	More difficult problems	207
	The values associated with e-portfolio tools and practices	210
	References and further reading	211
25	The culture of information and choice: an analogy with the development of agriculture	213
	References and further reading	217
26	In conclusion?	219
Glossary: Terminology, notes and abbreviations		221
Appendix: Personal development planning		233
Bibliography		237
Index		239

About the author

Simon Grant has been an information systems consultant for several years, and currently specialises in e-portfolios and their interoperability, with a strong forward interest in personal values and the technology that could be related to them. One of his main roles has been as a coordinator and adviser for CETIS, the Centre for Educational Technology and Interoperability Standards, in the e-portfolio area.

After his degree in physics and philosophy, he went into school-teaching, where his degree had conveniently provided a good basis for teaching physics. However, he didn't get along in a school system where he was expected, not to encourage much thinking, growth and diversity, but rather to keep order, and coax children through examinations in subjects that didn't really interest them. He has spent other periods as an educator, giving individual tuition, teaching at university (following a PhD), and training people in internet skills.

In parallel, he has had a long thread of interest, and some involvement, in the area of counselling and psychotherapy. He was a Nightline volunteer as a student. He trained briefly as a hypnotherapist, and practised that for a short time. Later, he did an introductory course in marital counselling with what was then London Marriage Guidance.

On 'big five' psychological measures he scores particularly high on what is often called 'openness'. He sees this as going along with not being bound by convention, but rather valuing growth and development, diversity and choice – valuing people exploring the world and themselves, and finding things and other people they really value, and perhaps love. He loves people who he can see growing and developing, and particularly he loves, in an attached and committed way, those people whose growth and development he can help with most.

He is a Quaker, a member of the Religious Society of Friends. Quakers also tend to try not to judge by appearance: they have an honourable tradition of treating people equally, irrespective of any status, or markers of status. Like him, Quakers are happy with questions, and draw back from putting answers into fixed forms of words. But many Quakers have deep faith and commitment nevertheless, and do good work. That's one tradition he is comfortable with.

The author may be contacted at:

E-mail: *asimong@gmail.com*
Website: *http://www.simongrant.org/home.html*

Acknowledgments

Many colleagues and friends have over the years given me the stimulus, the encouragement, and the feedback which are so vital for developing ideas such as these. Thanks to all of you, wherever you are. Some people have been particularly helpful in the areas discussed in this book, and I'd like to mention these people by name, and in a roughly chronological order. Most of them have also commented most helpfully on one or other part of the drafts for this book. The traditional formula fits well: I'd like to thank them warmly for their help, while taking personal responsibility for any faults that remain.

Janet Strivens, of the University of Liverpool, introduced me properly to this area of personal development as practised, and together we devised Liverpool's LUSID system in 1997, which offered a seminal opportunity for me to start off my thinking in this whole area. She is still a greatly valued colleague, and we work actively together on several projects.

Rob Ward, of the Centre for Recording Achievement, has offered great personal and career support, in the role of manager as well as colleague.

Helen Richardson has worked with me over several years in this area of e-portfolios.

I've known Oleg Liber, the director of CETIS, for several years, but I am particularly grateful that in the time that he has been my direct manager, he has taken an interest in my work, and counted my writing this book as a good thing to be doing in CETIS time.

Scott Wilson has been a key CETIS colleague when it has come to developing interoperability specifications. Almost always, if I want to know something rather more technical than I know, it will be Scott that has a sound and reliable view on the matter.

Darren Cambridge is now renowned in the area of electronic portfolios, and I am very glad to have had the opportunity to work with him since the IMS ePortfolio specification work and before.

Andrew Charlesworth, of the University of Bristol, has been involved in IT and law for many years, and I met him through his legal work for

JISC. He has given me valuable suggestions on legal matters in this book. Because he was responsible for employing her, he is also one of those indirectly responsible for my meeting my wife.

The others who could be held partly responsible, as they organised the event where we met, an e-portfolio conference in La Rochelle, are Serge Ravet and Maureen Layte of EIfEL, who have always been friendly and stimulating colleagues in the e-portfolio world.

Anna (née Home) is to be most heartily thanked for supporting my writing of this book, not only in being a loving wife, but also by helping me think through ethical matters, and anything and everything relating to the social sciences. Our paper on ethical portfolios was an inspiring early step on the road towards the thinking in Part 3.

Preface

With the possible exception of autistic people, we all care about the impressions of ourselves that are conveyed to others. Often, and for good reasons, we want to give different impressions in different situations, and to different people. Our actions, our words, our dress and appearance convey some impressions, as they have done for people for millennia. As technology has advanced, many other tools and media have started to play a part in this process. Writing offers a medium for composing CVs and other autobiographical material. Photography, audio and video recordings supplement, complement or may even replace the written word. Information and communications technologies, including today's social networking technology, not only make writings, images, and voice directly available to anyone with the appropriate connections, but also, increasingly, allow people to be purposefully selective about what they choose to read, view or listen to.

But what about the converse of that last point: how can we purposefully select the information presented about ourselves to others? To do that, we need to know three things: what information we might present, what people might be interested in, and how to present it. Each of these areas of knowledge can be developed. We can all develop our own knowledge of ourselves, within our own limits. Greater knowledge of what others are interested in, and of how to present that to them, potentially enables us to develop tailored presentations of ourselves. Properly tailored presentations give a better chance that, even when others are selective about the information they gather, the impression they gather will be the one we intend.

The technology developed to play a part in these processes could have many different names, but one term that happens to be used currently is 'electronic portfolio' (routinely abbreviated to 'e-portfolio'). The term 'portfolio' is associated, among other things, with the focused task of gathering and organising evidence, for assessment of whether a learner is competent in a particular field of knowledge or experience. In this book, when we discuss 'e-portfolios', we mean sets of materials selected by us to help in the presentation of ourselves to others in the way we choose.

An e-portfolio, then, is a product, and this implies process and practice, in other words, what is done in the course of, and leading up to, producing these e-portfolios for presentation. This practice may extend to cover personal reflection, collection of relevant information, organisation and management of that information, and its selection for presentation to others. Then there is the presentation itself, and, completing the cycle, receiving feedback and reflecting on that feedback.

Tools and systems with the label 'e-portfolio' may play a part at various stages of this process, and so may tools and processes with other labels or names, including 'social networking', 'personal development planning' (PDP), 'continuous professional development' (CPD), and several others. Different tools differ widely in the functionality they offer: the more helpful a tool or system is with these tasks, and the wider range of relevant tasks it covers, the more it makes sense for us to call it an 'e-portfolio tool' or 'e-portfolio system'.

This book is primarily about the principles behind the kinds of ICT tools and systems that can help with these processes and practices. It is also about the human processes, practices and systems that run alongside, and interface with, the use of the technology. It is concerned with the purpose, function and development of the technology and associated systems. The terminology used for the systems, tools and practices is of lesser importance, as it might well continue to change greatly.

Understanding more about the nature of this technology, about the systems that use it, and about the information that exists in these systems, can help different people in various ways. It can help us to use the tools to manage this kind of personal information about ourselves. It can help practitioners – teacher, tutor, counsellor, mentor, manager, to give some names for relevant roles – to help others to develop and know themselves with the help of the technology, and to improve the way they manage and present information about themselves. It can help those who develop related ICT systems to develop tools which serve people better. And lastly, it can bring insight to policy-makers who may be developing policy for the deployment of this kind of ICT.

1

Introduction

Guide for readers

Who are you, O reader? Depending on who you are, or really, at this point, what you are interested in, I'd like to point each of you to the parts of this book that are most relevant to you as individuals, but first I'll start by mentioning what the parts contain.

Part 1 contains a rationale for the systems and tools that are discussed in this book. It is important to have this rationale as a basis for understanding how to use and take forward the technology to good effect.

Part 2 contains structured notes on how to do things with the technology and tools related to e-portfolios, including useful questions to ask and actions to consider. This covers a range of concerns, from how to use e-portfolio tools for various purposes, through to how to build useful tools which work together. This part of the book is designed to be of direct use, to learners themselves, to those designing e-portfolio systems, and to those taking decisions or setting related policy.

Part 3 builds on what is established, looking forward towards future possibilities. This looks at our personal values, and how storing and managing the information about those values will enable greater real choice in our lives.

Back to you now. For the present, I assume you read English to a reasonably educated level. I imagine you have at least a little acquaintance with computer technology used for education or personal development; if not, it is enough that you are familiar with the ways that information and communication technologies are frequently used in this first decade of the twenty-first century. Beyond these assumptions, you may not want to classify yourself. You may even be most comfortable remaining anonymous. In that case, I give you the book as a whole: make what sense of it you can. I would particularly recommend Part 3, as it is forward-looking and potentially relevant to anyone who may be living in a future which is not very distant. Part 1 may serve as useful background to Part 3.

Beyond my general assumptions, there are particular kinds of readers that I do envisage. You may be a user of some e-portfolio system, and possibly classed as a 'learner', at whatever stage of learning. If so, my guess (and it can only be a guess at best) is that you might be interested in all of Part 1, as this will give you the background to understand why it may be that you are using e-portfolio tools. You might be interested in appropriate chapters of Part 2, though probably not all of them.

You may be a practitioner involved with e-portfolio technology; perhaps you are involved in personal or professional development, or careers information, advice and guidance. Depending on your level of knowledge and experience, you may be familiar with some of the issues presented in Parts 1 and 2. I hope that the book's synthesis of all the issues together is of some value to you. My hope is that the book will help to clarify your overview of the subject, and add depth to your appreciation of the issues. And I hope you will be able to take forward some of the vision in Part 3.

You may be a decision-maker – someone who can make decisions about strategy and policy for adopting e-portfolio and related tools, whether in education or in business. If so, I hope that Part 1 gives you a clear and useful overview of the issues involved, and that chapters in Part 2 answer some of your questions directly. Part 3 is my vision for the future. I would be delighted if this vision were to add a positive orientation to any decisions you might make that influence the future – ideally a future influenced positively by the kind of technology we are discussing.

You may have an interest in developing the kind of systems under discussion. If that description fits you, I hope that Part 1 will ensure that you have not overlooked any major areas of requirements; that some of the chapters in Part 2 will give you answers you can implement; and that Part 3 will help you develop systems and tools that inspire both your clients and the end users.

You may be a student of this technology, or just have a general interest in it. If so, I hope the book will help you towards many insights which will play a part in your deeper understanding of the whole area.

If we were to engage in a personal dialogue, then the more you told me about yourself, and the more that you responded to my questions about your motives, interests and requirements, the more I could point you directly to the relevant parts of this book. And where the book leaves off, as it must, we could take the conversation further.

The dialogue we could imagine between us parallels some aspects of using e-portfolio systems in practice. The more we know about each other, the richer is the possible interaction between us. We could, perhaps, imagine a future electronic version of something like this book. You would fill in a questionnaire, or just point to your own stored portfolio information, and then automatically receive relevant guidance on what you might want to know or need to know from this book. For now, however, the printed word will have to suffice...

E-portfolio systems: purpose, information, functionality

Over the years of study of and practice with e-portfolio systems and tools, three related issues, or dimensions, concerning e-portfolio systems have emerged as particularly helpful in thinking about them. First, there are the purposes for which a system is used; second, there is the information produced and used in conjunction with the system; and third, there is the system's functionality – that is, what its various users are allowed or enabled to do by the system. This three-way classification was developed working with colleagues in the e-portfolio area, and they have also found it helpful. Clarifying the boundaries and linkages between these issues saves people from the all too common problems arising from confusing them.

Starting with purpose, if you (a decision maker or policy maker perhaps) have a purpose in mind, perhaps an educational or development purpose, this may lead you on to the question of how you are intending to set about fulfilling that purpose. What tools do you, or might you, use for that purpose? What functionality is provided by these tools? And parallel to the consideration of tools, what information is relevant to these purposes?

Or instead, you could start from considering what personal information is held in your system, whether or not the system has the label 'e-portfolio'. In these days of taking data protection and privacy very seriously, it is important to understand why the information is being held, in other words, for what purpose? Any information that is gathered and stored may be put to some use, so how is your information used? Are some of the ways in which it is gathered, managed and used under the control of the person to whom the information refers? (This person will be called the 'portfolio holder' in this book). And what information do the tools make available to the portfolio holder, whatever those tools are called?

And last but not least, if you have tools or systems that deliver or provide functionality to users (that is, tools that allow your users or learners to do particular things), to what end can this functionality be used? What information can and do the tools handle?

These issues may seem a little abstract at first, but should be clearer after looking more at purposes, information and functionality in subsequent chapters. As the examples emerge, I hope how they fit together will become more clear.

The picture of e-portfolio systems that will emerge involves the interplay of these three aspects. Leave out any one aspect, and the picture loses clarity. Thus, I do not intend to provide a simple classification of portfolio systems in terms of any one aspect alone, but rather I will allow the definition to emerge implicitly from the consideration of all three together.

This same combination of the three issues is important also to answer practical questions. As we will see in Part 2, it is not helpful to tackle practical questions in terms that concern purpose, information or functionality alone.

What this book is not

This book is not a guide to policy for education or personal development – policy needs to respond to the context of a particular time and place. The subject matter of this book is meant to be independent of place, and, as much as can be hoped for, to be relatively enduring through time. Rather than advising directly on policy, this book deals with the some of the principles behind any policy relating to e-portfolio strategy, and thus may help to shape or inform policy.

It is not intended to be a review of current technology. While technology develops quickly, the principles underlying it change only relatively slowly. This book is designed to deal with the principles underlying the technology, although it will use examples of current technology to relate to these principles.

It is not a guide to pedagogical practice using e-portfolios – this topic is explored in a number of other books. Instead, this book deals with the principles underlying practice with this kind of technology, thus throwing extra light on the practice covered in other works.

This book does not contain case studies, but can be used to help to illuminate and to compose case studies. Case studies can too easily be written from just one perspective, leaving out detail which is vital for relating the case study to other perspectives. For a different approach to writing case studies, you can use this book as a guide to the variety of significant perspectives potentially relevant to case studies, making it more likely that a good range will be covered, and that case studies will be more generally useful and will relate to a greater range of stakeholders.

Another difficulty with case studies is that they date. The typical kinds of human challenge relating to portfolio use do not change much over time, so it makes sense for books about learning and development to set out typical and classic cases illustrating the kinds of process that need to happen in human terms. But the ways of meeting these challenges change rapidly, along with the technology that is available to support the processes. To be relevant to this book, case studies would have to include the particular, changeable, technology. All in all, it makes more sense to look for case studies elsewhere.

What is so personal?

Why does the book's title stress 'personal'?

First, e-portfolios deal in information that is personal, both in common understanding, and according to data protection law. Many people are interested in creating personalised education or other services, and this can only be done with personal information about individuals.

Second, one of the strengths of e-portfolio practice is that it allows people to assemble information about themselves in their own way, and present it in their own way. The concept of an e-portfolio is very different from a standard application form: standard forms constrain both the content and the structure of information supplied.

Third, personal development is personal in that it differs from person to person: everyone's personal development follows its own path, even though there are similarities and parallels.

Fourth, I will be discussing things that are personal in the sense of relating to personality, including personal values. This is covered mainly in Part 3.

So there is a strong connection between e-portfolio thinking and various 'personal' concepts. But the connections are not entirely obvious, and one of the tasks of this book is to clarify them.

References and further reading

Colleagues Rob Ward and Helen Richardson used the concepts of purpose, information and functionality in their series of guides to e-portfolio requirements, with titles starting 'Getting what you want...'. These guides are available electronically (e.g. see *http://wiki.cetis.ac.uk/Portfolio_requirements*) and are aimed at people in various roles in educational institutions.

Part 1:
Principles of e-portfolio systems

This first part of the book builds up and follows through a line of reasoning and explanation about the nature of e-portfolio systems. As introduced previously, the three interwoven aspects need to be explored and explained, in order to give a sound basis for the practical suggestions presented in Part 2. After some initial context in Chapters 2 to 4, Chapters 5 to 9 look first at purposes, then at information, then at functionality. Chapter 10 rounds this off by considering in outline how the three aspects support each other, using the example of a common area of application of e-portfolio tools: education.

2

Some scenarios of e-portfolio use

This chapter grounds the following argument and discussions with some examples generalised and perhaps extended a little from current practice and experience. The examples here are really just outlines, giving a flavour of the kind of things that happen at present.

Assessment

Avril is working towards a vocational qualification in audio-visual arts technology.

She is studying while at work, and following an e-learning course provided by a local college. The course is managed through what is officially referred to as a 'virtual learning environment' or a 'course management system', but in the college it has its own name. Avril can access the course material from any browser, wherever she is. For each course module, the assignments required for assessment are detailed within the system. On the current module, for one of the assignments, Avril needs to make a video describing and illustrating stop-motion animation techniques, using her own shots mixed with other freely-available material to illustrate the subject matter.

She adds her own voice-over commentary to the video, incorporating her reflections on the task.

She uploads the video to the system. Even over the broadband connection provided in her workplace, the ten-minute video takes some minutes to upload. Then she clicks on a button on the screen to indicate that she is happy with that version.

The next day, her workplace supervisor logs in to the system and finds Avril's new work. He indicates that Avril's work is authentic, and ready for assessment by the external assessor.

The next week, the external assessor assesses Avril's latest work, along with the work of several others, by viewing the video from her own computer over the web.

The following day, Avril is able to see that her latest work has been passed by the assessors. That box has been ticked, and she has already started on the next assignment. Her course continues following a similar repeated pattern.

Presentation for transition

Bart wants to move on from college to university. He has been studying English and maths, but has recognised that he doesn't want a career in journalism or writing, and is investigating a more technical career. He remembers that he used to enjoy building complex Lego houses as a boy, and he has heard from friends that construction engineering is a promising career area, so he goes to see his adviser in the college.

He has already previously been using his college's e-portfolio system to set goals, to work out an individual learning plan and to keep track of progress. One of the ways that progress is tracked is by results from diagnostic assessments being available through the system. This is a good reference point for discussion with advisers, as both sides know the information is available.

At one meeting, his adviser takes Bart through his latest results, and helps him to revise his plan accordingly. Bart's new plan includes mapping his achievements and skills against the requirements for entry to a construction engineering course. One of the entry requirements is a structured personal statement from the candidate. The e-portfolio system allows Bart's adviser, with his consent, to read through the material that Bart has collected which might be relevant to this personal statement, and at another meeting, they go through this together, discussing the virtues of mentioning various things in the statement.

In time, the personal statement is ready. Bart, with the help of his adviser, registers with the admissions service, and refers to the personal statement, stored in the college e-portfolio system, to complete the answers.

Later on, Bart discovers that he has been rejected. However, the application service has given informative feedback, and this is discussed along with his adviser. The adviser manages to keep Bart engaged, and helpfully suggests a range of alternative subjects, and together they decide on property management and surveying, which also has plenty of vacancies.

After a similar process, Bart's application is successful. When all the formalities are complete, as part of the induction process, Bart asks for the university e-portfolio system to retrieve the details he has stored on the college e-portfolio system. After reviewing which ones he wants to preserve, and which he would prefer to forget, he gives the command, and the selected information is transferred to his new place of study.

Development of skills in general

Dawn is an undergraduate student of computer science. In a meeting with her course adviser, she has identified that she may need to develop her communication skills, as she knows they are needed in many of the jobs she will be aiming for in 18 months' time.

She logs in to her university's e-portfolio system and gets to grips with the skills audit section. When looking over the communication skills audit, the system asks whether she has any evidence that her skills are adequate. She realises that she hasn't thought deeply about her communication skills, and has no evidence to back up her idea that she might be OK in that area. Perhaps she has more needs in this area, and needs to do more work on it. The college where she did her foundation degree did get her to do some e-portfolio work, and several of the experiences she recorded have appeared in her e-portfolio system at the university.

Over the next few days, she goes over the experiences she has recorded, and records on the system how much she thinks she used communication skills in each one. This process reminds her of other more recent experiences, which she also adds in and rates. The system offers her questions about different aspects of communication skills, so a couple of days later, she goes back to the site, filling in which experiences were good examples of these different aspects of communication.

Later again, returning to the summary of when she used communication skills in the past, she notes those aspects of communication skills for which she seems to have good evidence, and which less so. She e-mails her personal tutor, asking her to check the plausibility of her judgments about this. On receiving feedback from the tutor, she goes back to the system, which offers recommendations of self-study materials for improving the aspects she seems to have covered least. In one of the self-study guides, it suggests that the evidence for oral communication skills that will carry most weight with employers might come from her tutor observing her in group work. Using the portfolio system, she constructs a plan to do more self-study work, and to ask her tutor, next time he is observing her, to make notes that she can then use as evidence.

Learning to learn and reflect

Leo is a student nurse. He does not particularly enjoy academic work, but rather likes where he is, in a socially useful job where he works with people. However, he has to get through the coming exams for the course that he is following, in parallel with his work.

He has received feedback, which is available for viewing through the e-portfolio system, that his work is too descriptive and not sufficiently reflective to fit in with the new guidelines for nurse education.

Leo's course is well integrated with the e-portfolio system that they use. The course is based on a problem-based learning approach, and there is a strong emphasis on peer-group learning. The students have plenty of experience working together in groups. Even when members of the group are working on different placements, they are expected to continue communicating: the e-portfolio system doubles as a communication system.

While on placement, Leo is expected to note down critical incidents. The place on the system to make records of these includes space for:

- describing what happened;
- considering how to think differently about the incident;
- considering the perspectives of the different people involved;
- boxes to check when the record can be shared with fellow students and with the tutor.

Comments can be added by fellow students and tutors.

Leo is a bit puzzled by the feedback about not being reflective. He wonders what it really means. He starts looking back through his own records, and the comments on them. He notices that one of his fellow students, Sarah, has been asking a few questions in her comments on his work. Leo has just brushed these off before as they didn't make any sense to him. But looking at them again, he wonders if they might relate to this 'reflective' thing. He goes and looks at the records that she has made available to fellow students. 'Hmm, yes, her approach is different from mine,' he thinks, 'she seems to think a lot deeper than me'. He gets on his instant messenger service and, yes, Sarah is there. He asks if he can go round for a quick discussion...

When they talk, Sarah points out a few other fellow students that perform well in terms of reflection.

Later, Leo looks more at the critical incident reports written by the students mentioned by Sarah. After a few weeks trying new ways of thinking, Leo is doing much better with recording critical incidents, and getting more interested comments from fellow students, and better feedback from tutors.

Application for a job

Nadia works at a junior level for a large financial services business, badly hit by financial turbulence. Many staff will not be needed, and are being made redundant, and Nadia has been given two months' notice. Nadia joined the company three years ago. Although she has no degree, she has obvious natural flair. Her area of business is now being abandoned by the company, and the whole sector is suffering, so there is little chance of a straight move to another similar role, particularly with no higher-level qualification.

The company, trying unusually hard to look after its employees, has bought into an e-portfolio system designed to support employability. One feature of this system is that it takes whatever information is available from other business systems in the company, placing it all into a store of information relevant to future employability, CVs and the labour market. Employees can fill in the rest.

Nadia attends a briefing on this system given by one of the HR managers. She is introduced to her account on the system, and shown how the information from the HR system has already been added. The manager explains how the completed portfolio can be used both to generate a free-standing skills-oriented CV, and also how the information can be entered into recruitment systems. There is a good instruction manual on the corporate intranet, which she studies later to check up on what was introduced.

Over the next two days, she fills in what gaps she can on the system. Most of the information about her education is already there, as it was on the corporate HR system. The system also includes other useful things that were added while in this job, including material from her annual staff appraisal meetings. She can see that this will form the basis of evidence for many of the skills that she has developed with this company. In the section on her own requirements and ambitions she records that she wants a job that provides real support for higher education in the workplace, as well as the more usual expectations of industry sector, type of job, salary and location. She notices that there is more detail than in other systems she has seen before, and wonders what else to fill in.

Nadia makes an appointment with an HR adviser the following week. The adviser suggests some other kinds of job that Nadia has not previously considered. As the system provides for extra detail, Nadia asks about what she should fill in. The adviser agrees that it is a good idea not to ask for a family-friendly policy unless one is definitely thinking of starting a family soon. The adviser takes Nadia through the process of uploading information from the e-portfolio system into the national employment matching service, but it doesn't come out with any good opportunities. Nadia will have to keep trying, and keep thinking about any extra helpful information she could put into the e-portfolio system.

After another couple of weeks, Nadia has found a potential job and been asked for interview. She looks carefully at the job requirements, and notes that she needs to think about how to answer questions at interview, particularly concerning her capacity to learn and effectively use complex, high-level concepts.

When she starts in the new job, she uses the portfolio tool to authorise the transfer of most of the information recorded about her to her new employer's HR and training management system. It will help in her progress towards her chosen degree.

References and further reading

There is nowhere obvious to go for any collections of example scenarios like these. Perhaps the best way forward is to look at the literature surrounding the use of e-portfolio tools in various contexts. From this, one may be able to construct similar scenarios and also understand more about the background behind them.

3

Who wants personal information?

The examples in the last chapter are generalised from current practice, mixed in with some ideas that are well on their way to being recognised as established. These are some of some of the reasons why people engage in activities involving e-portfolio systems. To get a more rounded and complete view, it would help to examine the general motives or purposes for all this effort that people are putting into collecting and using this kind of information about themselves, their knowledge and their skills.

We can perhaps start from the general observation that what you want is partly influenced what you are entitled to – this is as much true for information as for other things. Leaving aside legal entitlements, which are best dealt with in a legal context, the assumption made here is that you are entitled to record information and history that is relevant to yourself, for your personal use. In free societies, individuals are allowed to record any personal reflections on just about anything. Restrictions normally only come into play when passing information on to other people. Businesses and other organisations are expected, and may be required, to keep records of their transactions with individuals and with other businesses or organisations. What they can do with information about individuals is governed by data protection legislation. This is discussed further in Chapter 7.

The fact that data protection legislation exists points to the wider significance of personal information: if we didn't feel that information was significant, there would be little motivation for legislation. Perhaps one of the most significant roles of personal information is that it underpins communications in general. What we say to someone depends vitally on how we see that person: what their role is, what they know already, how they can be influenced. We will start to explore this further by looking at the categories of people who might want personal information.

Ourselves

We are the people most obviously entitled to know and use information about ourselves. Although no one could deny that, it may sometimes appear that there are obstructions. Some organisations in particular may prefer you not to know what they know about you, and perhaps occasionally what they know about you is more than you are aware that they know, or what you would want them to know.

There are several good reasons why we may want to store personal information about ourselves. First, we may want to store it because our memories are not good enough to remember reliably all that is relevant to something we are trying to do. Most people remember basic personal details such as their own name and address well enough, but the ever-increasing demands of society, as well as the workplace, dictate that no one can realistically remember accurately everything that they have a good reason to.

Second, although many people still use some form of paper records, we may want to use more advanced technology to help us manage the stored records. In everyday life, one obvious example is the storage and management of photographs. People have taken and kept photographs ever since cameras have been available, but storage in physical albums has limitations. New ways of storing digital photographs enable people to perform effective searches of the kind that can be infuriatingly difficult when limited to a single organisation scheme, whether that scheme is chronological or thematic.

Third, the act of recording may be part of another important process. Whenever writing materials have been available, some people have kept diaries, and while some diaries somehow manage to be mere lifeless records of disjointed facts (ones that I have written come to mind), in others it is clear that the act of recording has resulted in the creation of something really interesting. We could say something similar about photographic, audio and video recording. We can see every act of recording as an act of selection from the stream of lived experience, and what is selected is significant. Another approach to recording is the rather old-fashioned practice of making scrapbooks. Here, the act of choosing something is even more clearly significant than it is with diaries. Why keep one particular newspaper cutting, one might ask? Now, with the web, a similar question could be, why bookmark that page, or, why make a copy of that particular document?

Surprisingly perhaps, there have been no major initiatives to combine portfolio information with personal information as it is thought of in terms of 'personal information management', which is usually related to calendars, contacts and the like. I expect this will change when people recognise the potential explored in Part 3.

Educators

Educators may want to know various things about the learners to whose education they are contributing, depending on their degree of engagement with those learners, and the degree of personalisation of their learning processes and opportunities. Some of the things that educators want to know may be the kinds of thing that we envisage appearing in electronic portfolios.

At the disengaged and impersonal end of the spectrum, we might imagine educators preparing e-learning materials for a global audience. They know nothing in particular about their students, other than the presumed fact of their engagement with the learning materials. Assumptions may be made, but no personal information is involved.

A traditional lecturer in a college or university may know something in general about their students, but there are few occasions for one-to-one interaction in a large lecture theatre, so personal information is unlikely to be significant in that context. Naturally, any good lecturer uses the non-verbal response from their audience as a whole, which might give them a clue about whether a point made came across as obvious or obscure, interesting or boring. On the other hand, admissions tutors will want to know, in general terms, that the students have reached a suitable level of attainment to benefit from the course.

However, the classroom teacher or tutor for an individual or group is likely to build up more knowledge about their own students, and this knowledge can arise from the educational process itself. The teacher is certainly likely to be interested in what individuals do or do not understand, what they have mastered, and what they have not yet attained. Teachers who are closely involved with learners in the longer term are in a good position to keep this in mind, and use it to good effect, through long-term engagement with particular learners. But what of situations where the engagement is short term? Many teachers will have come across situations where they would like to know more about a particular pupil. What is the pupil's personal situation? What things should *not* be said to that individual, for personal reasons? What motivates that person? What are their personal interests and aspirations? What is their personal learning style? What causes a particular child to be disruptive in class? Perhaps the most committed educators really want to get a grasp of what 'makes them tick'. To have answers to these kinds of question would undoubtedly make a teacher's task, which is always challenging, more manageable. It would also allow educators to achieve more personalisation for their learners.

You cannot easily acquire this personal knowledge from the kind of information filled in on forms. It normally only comes through extended personal interaction – but this is resource-intensive. One might be able to get some personal knowledge from looking at an individual's interactions with others through social software, and how they put themselves across to others in various contexts, and this may be less expensive. But interestingly, from the perspective of this book, much of this kind of knowledge can be related to the information that people might store in electronic portfolio systems as a result of exercises in personal development and reflection.

From the examples in the previous chapter, perhaps Bart illustrates this best. In his desire to change his area of study when moving on to university, he gathers together information useful to himself, useful to his adviser in helping him make his decisions, and potentially useful for admissions staff in the university, trying to understand what kind of a person he is.

Employers

Perhaps it would be possible to represent the interests of employers as falling between two ends of a spectrum. At one end, an employer could regard an employee as a valuable resource, and they have an interest in personal information just as much as with information about any valuable resource. At the other end, employees could be seen as human beings whose interests should be looked after, and who should be helped to reach their full potential.

The position at the first end of the spectrum, not very far perhaps from the ideas of 'scientific management', Taylorism and Fordism, fits in well with the phrase 'human resources'. If employees are seen as the vehicles for competent performance of jobs, they may need training to improve their competence. To serve this, the employer, and particularly the employer's HR department if there is one, may want to know about the employee's competences – knowledge, skills, aptitudes, personality perhaps – anything which affects work performance either individually, or in teams.

HR-XML (*http://www.hr-xml.org/*) is an organisation that develops and promotes common XML standards, also known as HR-XML, for use in the HR industry, so its definitions are of interest here. HR-XML defines a competency as:

> a specific, identifiable, definable, and measurable knowledge, skill, ability and/or other activity-related characteristic (e.g. attitude, behaviour, physical ability) which a person can possess and which is necessary for, or material to, the performance of an activity within a specific context.

In the position at the other end of the spectrum, the employer's concern with the development of individual employees as people could be seen as quite close to the position of the ideal educator. But is this appropriate? Some people might see it as paternalist and unnecessarily invasive, particularly if employees view their work as a purely contractual sale, for money, of time spent competently on the job. But if employees see the workplace as more like a home – a view perhaps encouraged by some employers and preferred by many employees – then personal development would seem quite appropriate.

There are many middle positions along the spectrum, where, for example, the enlightened self-interest of the employer leads to their taking some interest in the development of individual employees, either because this is seen by employers as an attractive aspect of their terms or conditions, which they can use in recruitment for attracting good applicants; or because it is a way of making employees happier, and therefore more productive, and less liable to take time off sick, or to leave for another employer.

Public agencies

Public agencies have a more strictly circumscribed relationship with the citizens with which they interact. Public revenue services, for example, want only to know about your financial affairs, and of that, only about what incurs taxation, or qualifies for relief. Passport agencies want only to know about relevant matters such as identifying information, nationality and residence. Information-gathering in these contexts, for these agencies, is well encapsulated by the forms we commonly fill in when interacting with them (whether paper or electronic).

We have already dealt with educators, and educators in many countries are employed by national or local government. Other agencies which might be interested in a more holistic view of the individual are those dealing with the health and welfare of children, and those helping with careers and employment, which may or may not be tied in some way to benefits. The more holistically public agencies treat their citizens, the more motivation there is for joining up the information held by different agencies, and this applies whether the agencies genuinely aim to look after people, or, perhaps, are more interested in spotting terrorists or other activists or dissidents.

It is therefore no surprise that political considerations are seen as highly relevant to questions of public holding of personal information. This book will not attempt to go into political questions, beyond one high-level observation here. Some neo-liberals may believe it is none of the state's business worrying about child development or employment, as these belong to the private domains of family and individual responsibility. These people may also minimise the importance of state involvement in education. By contrast, the social-liberal position, which entails some kind of concept of the welfare state and safety nets, implies a greater involvement, and thus more reason to know personal information.

Friends and the peer group

The recent rise in the popularity of web-based social networking tools brings to the fore the question of personal information for 'use' by friends and family. I put 'use' in quotes because it seems more natural in other contexts to think of friends and family as having an 'interest' in personal information, rather than 'using' it. On the other hand, because we might say we 'use' social networking websites, the idea of 'using' information from those sites does not sound entirely inappropriate.

What kinds of things might you want to know about your friends, or potential friends? A starting point might be a desire to know who else they are friends with. Any social networking system can at least answer that, within its own system. From personal experience, this seems to be one of the first things of interest when looking up a friend on such a site. This could be to see how many friends they have, or to see whether they have someone you know as a friend.

Another piece of relevant information could be common interests – music, religion, sport or who knows what. Thus, a social networking site could provide the opportunity for people with shared interests to find one another. We also seem to be fascinated by how similar or different we are from others we know, and rating ourselves or others on many different scales.

It is not difficult to add speculations from your own experience, which may or may not actually have been tried. For example, you could record your dietary preferences so that your friends have easy access to them. If many friends did this, it would be easier to plan meals involving those friends. Alternatively, there may be value in being able to alert friends and family when someone dies, so that as many as possible can attend a funeral.

At present, we record these things about ourselves, and look at similar information about friends and acquaintances, but there seems to be much unused potential use for this information. We'll come back to this in Part 3.

References and further reading

HR-XML (2007) 'Competencies (measurable characteristics)', available at: *http://ns.hr-xml.org/2_5/HR-XML-2_5/CPO/Competencies.html*.

4

The rationale behind recording and storing personal information

In the discussion of who is interested in personal information, we have touched on some reasons why it should be stored electronically, rather than passed directly to other people as the occasion arises. Here we can bring these points together, taking a deeper look at purposes, together with examples of the information that is involved with those purposes.

Allowing others access to our information

The example of social networking highlights perhaps the most straightforward reason to make available information about ourselves. This is not unlike putting your name in the telephone directory: to allow people to find the information when you are not there to give it to them in person, or simply to save your personal time. This recognises the fact that people want information at different times, to suit themselves. It is also similar in principle to the motivation associated with the term 'Web 2.0', where the idea is to allow others access to any information we hold (not necessarily personal), and to use it in ways, as well as times, that we do not envisage in advance. When information is left open for others to retrieve and use, we are not controlling the presentation of that information. As such, the concern about possible misuse arises, and the issue of privacy becomes important, along with the need to be able to restrict the viewing of information to those who we have granted permission. Perhaps your telephone number, like mine, is now 'ex-directory', in an attempt to reduce unwanted calls.

Reuse across time and context

Perhaps one of the most straightforward examples of reusing information is with our own contact details: name, postal address, e-mail address, telephones, etc. There are already some ways of doing this; for example, my web browser stores various details about me, and offers to fill in the information on forms that come up on web pages.

Contact details are one of the most reusable pieces of personal information, but even there, we do not necessarily want exactly the same information in every context. Every new site requires a review of which contact details are appropriate to give to that site. People often have different e-mail addresses and different phone numbers for different purposes.

Another frequently used set of information is CV details, which people have put together and reused for decades. CV information taken together needs more customisation than is needed when the information is requested in smaller chunks. For years, the standard advice has been to produce a specific CV tailored for each different application, although the custom of putting CVs on employment websites tends to defeat that objective.

Coordinating permissions

Another reason for storing information electronically adds an extra dimension to the last example. If you have decided which information is to be given to which other people on which occasions, an electronic system allows those rules to be stored and programmed into the system, so the appropriate information can be given without the need to consult the portfolio holder on every occasion.

Communicating separately with each individual with whom you come into contact can be pleasant, and even rewarding, but is certainly more time-consuming.

A related example, familiar to many people, would be the circular letters you may send or receive, typically in December. The labour-intensive option is to consider, for each friend or family member, just what family news they might be interested in, and write that into the message sent to them. Instead, some people adopt the strategy of sending the same message to many people, whether printed or by e-mail. I have sometimes had the feeling, 'am I interested in this?', while the news that I was really interested in may have been left out on the grounds that there is someone it should not be shared with.

We can imagine an improvement on this, although it would be unlikely to be realised in practice. Each piece of information could be categorised (e.g. children, holidays, careers, extended family, etc.), and you could record which categories (you think) would interest each recipient. The task of at least partially personalised communication would then be rather easier: each piece of new information would be categorised, and any new recipients could be assigned categories of information. The rest could work automatically: when it comes to sending the news, the right information is printed out for each of your friends.

Then again, think of information about your dietary habits. Perhaps you want to let some of your friends know you now eat fish again, but you don't want to inform the whole world about that. As you would have already set the permissions, that information could be shared automatically with the same people who were permitted to see the information in the first place. This could probably be done in some social networking tools, but I haven't personally seen it yet.

Recording helps self-knowledge

Reliable self-knowledge is not attained easily. Socrates may have said that the unexamined life is not worth living, but equally it is clear that examining your life can be challenging. For instance, consider the challenge of reaching a reasonable judgment of how competent you are at a task or job, or how good you are generally at a particular skill. It has been noted that people are not naturally good at making objective assessments of their own level of ability, particularly when they are less than fully clear what that ability is expected to include, and when they do not have much experience of using that ability in practice. To get around this, recording episodes in which you practised or demonstrated a particular ability can help to lessen subjective bias. When asked about how good you are, you could refer back to those episodes to get a truer self-estimate.

Bearing particular people in mind when recording information about yourself seems likely to stimulate reflection on what it is that they might want to know, and this in turn serves to validate the usefulness of recording that information.

Furthermore, it could be argued that the act of deliberate recording (as opposed to automatic recording) serves to stimulate people's reflective capacity. A habit of recalling the happenings of the last day, or week, enables those things to be reflected on, even if they are not recorded.

5

Portfolio purposes outlined

Earlier chapters have introduced some of the ways that e-portfolios might be used. Before moving on to a more detailed consideration of portfolio information and portfolio functionality, it seems appropriate to draw together these considerations into a coherent summary. To formulate this as a question, what purposes might be served by e-portfolios as presentation documents, and by the e-portfolio systems that provide the functionality (to be discussed in more detail further below) that allows information to be collected, selected, reflected on, and presented as e-portfolios?

Just as personal information can be used in innumerable ways, so can e-portfolio systems be useful in all kinds of manner. To have any sensible discussion about the ends to which e-portfolio systems might be used it is useful to start by scoping out the kinds of purposes we may be discussing. The two starting points I propose here are, first, to identify the purposes of present systems; and second, a general consideration of plausible purposes. From these starting points, a few of the more obvious purposes will be spelled out, including the common ones noted above.

First, then, dealing with what is done at present, much recent literature tends to distinguish (approximately) four purposes:

- (formal, summative) assessment;
- self-presentation;
- supporting learning (possibly through formative assessment);
- supporting personal development (often involving self-assessment).

These have been illustrated in the scenarios in Chapter 2, but will be integrated into a more general framework here.

Second, in contrast, and more generally, we can start from the obvious and straightforward idea that portfolio systems, particularly electronic ones, exist to allow storage, retrieval and reuse of personally-related information. Here it is pertinent to identify who it is that reuses the information, thereby revealing a range of purposes, from those relating to one's own reuse of the information to those relating to other people's reuse of the information. In between, there are purposes involving reuse of the same information by oneself and by others.

Purposes which involve reuse of the information by oneself can be thought of as pertaining to reflection. Certainly, reflection aimed at your personal or professional development must involve you in recalling information relating to yourself, your achievements and your ambitions.

Purposes which involve the reuse of the information by others are not focused on personal reflection, although they may use the products of that reflection. Instead, the emphasis is often on the presentation of the information to others, as with CVs; alternatively, the emphasis could be on the sharing of information, such as your address, as discussed above, or for administrative purposes.

A little more significance in this distinction comes from considering how it mirrors the psychological contrast between introvert and extravert. Introverts may naturally prioritise the first kind of purpose, where portfolio holders reflect on information they have stored. Extraverts, in contrast, may naturally prioritise the use of stored information by, or for, other people. Having said that, explicit purposes are likely to be determined by the situation, more than by personality, and in any case, people are spread across a continuum between extraversion and introversion.

Purposes will be described relatively briefly, as the point is to identify and list purposes rather than to explore them.

Reflective purposes

In educational circles there is much talk of the 'reflective practitioner', although reflective practice is not much discussed in everyday life, and it is challenging to maintain a reflective attitude. This is highly relevant to e-portfolio technology, as there are obvious ways in which the technology can support reflection. Initially, any suitable and easy-to-use input device can be linked to storage, for example, to provide the facility for noting down thoughts as they occur. Subsequently, an ICT-based system can lead people through reflection in a structured way, prompting them to reflect on things that have happened.

No wonder, then, that many people in the fields of personal and professional development, who understand the value of reflection, have taken up the cause of portfolio tools to help people develop in their capacity for reflection, and to help their personal and professional development through the practice of reflection.

Below are two more specific and understandable purposes, both of which are clearly reflective.

Helping people to understand themselves, potentially to manage their lives better

This could be seen as a key top-level reflective purpose. People often need help to understand their own situation in life, their character, motives and interests, to move forward positively in their life and work. Beyond its obvious appeal to individuals, helping people understand themselves could be a valuable goal or target for personal networks, or for support agencies, which have an interest in people managing their own lives more effectively.

E-portfolio tools can facilitate the kind of reflection that helps people understand themselves better. Part 3 shows how this self-understanding could be extended to include personal values, using more advanced e-portfolio tools.

Supporting individual learning, development and planning

Planning to achieve your goals by yourself can also be seen as being essentially connected to reflection. Once your goals become sufficiently clear – as soon as you initially define them, in fact – it becomes possible for you to start planning to achieve them. The clarity of your goals in personal development is likely to increase as a result of greater self-understanding.

Purposeful personal development normally involves setting yourself goals or targets. Later reflection on whether those goals have been achieved, or targets met, is likely to lead in turn to greater personal insight and knowledge, contributing further to individual personal development. At least, that is the view that forms the basis of this purpose for e-portfolios.

What is called 'formative' assessment is closely related. This is also called 'assessment for learning' as opposed to 'assessment of learning'.

Purposes focusing on information use by others

The two main purposes in this category are given below.

Presentation to others

To present some information about ourselves to other people is a purpose shared by many of us. It is very unlikely that we would seriously want to present all the information about ourselves to everyone else, so in carrying out this purpose, we need either to make selections of our information, or to select our audience, or most likely both.

The material which is to be presented can be collected and selected using an e-portfolio system, and if the system allows this, it can be made available to others using that same system. If the system doesn't allow the information to be presented to our intended audience, we can transmit the selected information in some other way, perhaps by e-mail.

This purpose of presentation covers a wide range of situations, like applying for a job, a course or an award. Unlike formal summative assessment, other presentation tasks are generally open to the portfolio holder's personal approach and decision. The scenario of Bart in Chapter 2 illustrates this.

Formal 'summative' assessment

Submitting evidence or material to be assessed could well be part of a greater purpose which includes presenting the result of the assessment to other people. However, in our present society, it is very common to want to gain qualifications without necessarily knowing in advance how qualification information is going to be passed on, to whom, and why.

Material to be presented for assessment is normally specified either by the people undertaking the assessment, or by those managing the overall process of awarding the qualification. Because the process of awarding qualifications needs to be monitored and validated, it is common to use a specialised assessment portfolio system for this purpose. Such systems are not usually designed to allow presentation of that same information to people more widely.

The scenario involving Avril in Chapter 2 is closely related to this.

Purposes spanning use by ourselves and others

These two contrasting ways of using portfolio information – by ourselves for reflection, and to present to others – do not by themselves complete the picture. There is a limit to what we naturally do by ourselves, or what we can motivate ourselves to do, or what we have the skill or presence of mind to do. Many purposes blend together our own reflection alongside presentation to others, often with feedback from those others. This is most obvious in cases where the other people have an interest in our wellbeing or development. Below is my attempt to identify particular purposes that fall in this intermediate category.

Supported personal development

In our present society, personal development is often supported formally as well as informally by educational institutions, in addition to the personal development which naturally occurs as a part of family and other social life. Educational institutions covering all ages and stages have an interest in this. The institution is interested in the individual successfully completing whatever course of education they are involved in, and progressing to a satisfactory next stage, whether in education, employment, or life in general. This may be because the people involved in educational institutions value the development of their learners in any case, or less idealistically because the reputation and appeal of the educational institution depends in part on the visible success of their alumni.

Of the scenarios in Chapter 2, the most closely related ones here are those of Dawn and Leo.

Similar considerations would apply to other agencies such as public employment services, social services and prison services. It is in the interests of the public, or other stakeholders, that clients of those agencies progress to greater measures of self-reliance, usually involving employment. Many aspects of personal development are relevant to the ability to secure an appropriate job.

Employability and employee development

When in a job, it makes sense for employees to take into account their own continuing employability, whether with their present employer, or for a potential new one. If they want to retain their employees, their employers will also have common cause in wanting them to be employable. Even if redundancy is looming, a responsible employer will want to do something to help the outgoing employees to gain employment elsewhere, as was envisaged in the case of Nadia in Chapter 2.

Professional development

This is typically either offered by professional bodies, or required of their members. It is seen as encompassing many possible activities, and may or may not involve portfolio tools.

The individual may wish, for instance, to advance their career, to learn new skills to broaden the interest in their job, or to maintain their reputation as a professional. The professional body may be interested in prospering through attracting greater membership prepared to pay fees, so it needs to offer attractive, appropriate benefits to its membership. The more its members develop as professionals, the more the reputation of the professional body as a whole is likely to be enhanced.

Life coaching and executive coaching

Individuals may engage and pay for a life coach on their own initiative. It may be that you want to develop your career, in which case the costs might be outweighed by the possible increases in salary. A coach may deliver a service where you don't need to keep a portfolio, but the coach keeps records instead. The coach would be expected to provide the knowledge, skills and experience to help your development as an individual. The reputation, and thus income, of the coach will depend on the success of their clients.

In the case of executive coaching paid for by a company, any information stored (by the individual or coach), as well as being of use to a coach in the process of coaching, may also be of interest to the individual's employer. The relationship with portfolio technology may not be as simple as in the above cases. If you are a busy executive, you may not see it as a priority to take responsibility for maintaining your own records of your development. You may prefer that the coach deals with any recording – indeed you may see it as part of what you pay for.

Employee development

The purposes of employee development can be seen as a mixture of the employer's goal of improving the knowledge, skills, abilities, competences, etc. relevant to the employee's work, together with the employee's aim of developing themselves, which may go beyond the span of any particular employment. The concept is intended to include all employees, rather than just senior staff, and so it would be unusual to see the same resources devoted to this as to executive coaching. This could be turned to an advantage, as the employee is more likely to be required to keep records, which may in turn be beneficial.

Motivation is a challenge for any personal, professional or career development, but perhaps with employee development it is even more of a challenge than for the other cases, because of the relative difficulty for both parties in appreciating the benefits of the process. The issue of motivation is taken up shortly below.

Ancillary or related purposes

If we can see all of the above purposes as potential top-level goals, we can then imagine a process of breaking down these goals into sub-goals, and sometimes it will make sense to treat sub-goals as goals in their own right. One reason for breaking down top-level goals would be planning coherent interventions by bodies that support individuals. To use e-portfolio tools to achieve one or more of the purposes above, we can start by breaking down those higher-level purposes into some of the following lower-level ones, which are easier to grasp and focus on individually.

Planned interventions are situated in real contexts, and it would not be surprising if different contexts are associated with different lower-level purposes. Nevertheless, some of these ancillary purposes seem likely to arise across several contexts, and these are unpacked here.

One theme that recurs in studies of e-portfolio use is motivation. Building an e-portfolio system is one thing; persuading people to use it is another. It seems to be an accepted reality that the majority of students in higher-education contexts only engage with e-portfolio tools if their use is required or assessed as part of a course result. Whether or not this is a good way of motivating people, compulsion is not possible in other contexts. We will briefly consider here a few of the subdivisions of the motivation issue, followed by other ancillary purposes relating to e-portfolio tools.

These purposes may need to be addressed in order to ensure the effectiveness of e-portfolio systems. They could be pursued through whatever educational processes are normally available, but particularly if the portfolio system is provided for independent use, it would make sense to fulfil as many of these purposes as possible in conjunction with the tool itself.

Motivating reflection

To get people to engage with the reflective purposes of e-portfolio practice may require some extra motivation for what may be an unfamiliar and challenging process. This may not be so much of a problem if there is extrinsic motivation, such as a course requirement, for undertaking reflective exercises.

One approach may be to help people understand the nature of reflection, and how it is done. We may need help to reflect on experiences, achievements, or other things. Suitable introductory materials may provide stimulus and guidance. Exercises may be 'scaffolded'. Many approaches can be incorporated into the portfolio tool, or the material surrounding its use.

Motivating goal setting and action planning

Personal development planning (PDP) is frequently one of the ways in which e-portfolio tools are used in education, because of the expectation, in higher education at least, that PDP will be provided. An important component of PDP is action planning, which depends on having set goals. But what if a student is unconvinced of the value of these? Can we explain what the advantages are, so that students are properly motivated?

One way of doing this would be to present case studies of goal setting and action planning, to illustrate how they have been effective in other people's lives. Again, it is not difficult to imagine this approach being built into portfolio tools.

Motivation to use the portfolio tool

An individual may be motivated in other ways, but if the tool itself is not right for them, it may still be an obstacle to the fulfilment of the higher purposes. Tool motivation has positive and negative aspects. Positively, developers can try to make the use of the tool fun, enjoyable, or stimulating in itself. The tool must be easy to learn and highly usable. Negatively, they can try to avoid things which put people off: bad interface design would be a key issue here. More detailed discussion belongs to the field of usability.

Educating about potential dangers

If educational institutions are promoting the storage of personal information, they should at least be responsible for educating learners about potential dangers. Might the information fall into the hands of someone who could misuse it? While you are using an e-portfolio system, can you be tricked into thinking you are giving someone your own personal information legitimately, when in reality it is being stolen? (This is the essence of what is known as 'phishing'.)

This ancillary purpose arises from good practice considerations, rather than from an inherent necessity. It is not unreasonable to suppose that much can be accomplished just by providing the relevant information, in which case it could easily be built into a portfolio tool.

Providing relevant learning experiences

In the above discussion about purposes, one can see several opportunities to educate people about personal information, and this education may well help to motivate the use of e-portfolio tools, and allay fears about them. In this context, it includes learning any relevant skills, learning how to reflect, learning how to do action planning, and many other things.

There is no particular reason why any relevant learning experiences should not be presented in the normal way that any learning experience is presented in the context in question. But as an alternative, portfolio tools may themselves be designed, in part at least, to provide these learning experiences.

Of particular interest are those learning experiences that lead to learners improving their knowledge or skills, as these are linked to other natural portfolio purposes. A reflection on a lack of skill may motivate people to acquire it, and the possession of a skill may lead to a desire to present evidence of that skill to others. But the functions of providing these learning experiences are in principle no different from the functions of providing any other learning experiences.

Educating about what others may want

The effective use of a portfolio tool to present information to others will depend on a reasonable grasp of what information is of interest to those others. If this is not understood, the risk is that portfolio presentations will be ignored. Employers, clients, customers, organisers of higher-level courses and the like – all may want some portfolio information, but not necessarily the same things.

Careers guidance and similar services should provide general guidance about what is wanted 'in the real world' in terms of knowledge, skills, competence, etc. As well as what is actually wanted, it is important to know about what evidence is required, and what information can constitute that evidence.

This is a hugely significant area, which is arguably under-represented in current education. It could be seen as a core part of personal development, and is clearly linked to all kinds of advice and guidance, mentoring, life coaching, etc. It is also difficult to envisage how to use a portfolio tool for this purpose. However, an associated social networking system could be of benefit.

Education in self-presentation

How to present yourself to others is closely related to understanding what they want to know. But there is also much to learn about how to present the information in a pleasing way. People who are not so experienced, or not naturally so talented at self-presentation may need help here.

Again, it is hard to see this, or the following purpose, being fulfilled by portfolio tools for individuals by themselves; rather, a portfolio system would need to provide communication with others, at the very least.

Educating for evidence provision

What counts as evidence may not be obvious to everyone. Again, this is related to the question of what other people want to know. What evidence can be presented to whom, and how can it be provided? The other side to this is to learn about what achievements, artefacts and other things can reasonably be used as evidence.

Providing information, advice and guidance about knowledge and skills

What knowledge and skills are needed in any particular chosen area of life? If we know the answer to that, we are better able to plan our learning, which may involve e-portfolio tools. Once we have taken on the goal of improving something about ourselves, we need to know practical and sensible ways to reach that goal. This is something that should be easy enough to provide within a tool.

Purposes of others

Human groups, organisations and institutions can also have various purposes, some of which might relate to e-portfolio tools. It is worth remembering these other stakeholders, as well as ourselves. We can assemble a list of stakeholders from considerations in previous chapters. These may include individuals, families (as social and economic units), individual educators, educational institutions, companies, other organisations, and the state and its agencies.

References and further reading

A large amount of writing on the 'reflective practitioner' and 'reflective practice' can easily be found on the web by searching with those terms. Many people, writers and practitioners, refer to the work of Christopher Johns, Donald Schön and Chris Argyris; searching on their names is fruitful. The questions of motivation will be explored from a different perspective in Part 3.

6

Portfolio information

Having traced out what purposes can be served by portfolio tools, placing the tools in the context of human activity, we can now focus more on the second of the three major aspects of portfolio analysis: information. Because portfolio tools are built using information and communications technology (ICT), understanding their essence involves clarifying the kinds of information that they deal with. Many examples have already been mentioned in passing, but this chapter's task is to bring together a view on what information is naturally and properly involved with portfolios.

For educators, or others who help in people's learning and development, there may be something different about how the term 'information' is used here. When we think of information, the easiest image to bring to mind is of facts – in this case, perhaps facts about the person we are trying to help. But e-portfolio systems may serve to record much more than that, including work done by the learner, their opinions, reflections – in fact anything that might be recorded. All of these kinds of information are the subject of this chapter.

The chapter takes three views: first, historical and current practice of what information has been and is handled; second, considering information from the perspective of its purpose; and third, a more philosophical but still practical view of the nature of the information itself. Following this threefold view of the origins and nature of the information, the chapter goes on to assemble a list of types of information based on all three approaches.

Historical and current practice

Much of past and present practice using ICT grew out of older paper-based methods. The term 'portfolio' has for a long time been used in conjunction with creative activities such as writing, art and design. This kind of portfolio was originally a container for examples of one's work (that is, the 'folio') to carry around (that is, the 'port') and show to people. This practice has been readily adapted for assessment, as seen by the requirement for candidates to collect evidence of their abilities and present it in a (physical or electronic) portfolio. So, actual work done, or documentation of it, has always constituted a part of many portfolios. Educational practice then developed into requiring candidates not only to select and present the works themselves, but also to give some account of their creation, and to provide written evidence of the educational process and outcomes that were intended to go alongside the development of creative talent. Although originally conceived as enriching the set of materials for assessment, requiring this kind of evidence now also helps deter copying or plagiarism, which has become increasingly easy with the spreading availability of electronic resources and communications. In these ways, some kinds of reflective writing have become established as part of the information that is typically contained in a portfolio.

This is effectively what happens in much vocational education, and the example of Avril in Chapter 2 is illustrative.

Another strand of relevant historical practice has been the CV or résumé. Here, we typically see a selection of brief records of work and of education, lists of projects undertaken or authored works, lists of abilities, skills or competences, ambitions, and personal details including contact details. Student or personnel records kept either by educational institutions or by employers may include, but go beyond, these CV details.

A third strand of historical practice has been personal and professional development. Professional development tends to have a reasonably clear definition of what information is relevant to it, including such things as which exams have been passed, which certificates obtained, which professional grades have been accomplished or are still being sought, evidence of skill and competence, records of experience in roles, and professional development activity such as attending courses, workshops seminars etc. Initial professional development may help a new professional adopt appropriate professional standards and codes of practice or ethics, while there is a continuing dimension related to keeping up with developments in the professional field, as well as progressing one's own career. This tends to be situated within a professional development framework of some kind, which, as well as setting out what is necessary to maintain professional status, may also allow people to select their own goals, and the actions that lead towards achieving those goals.

Personal development may not be so clearly scoped, and the information relevant to it is correspondingly less well-defined. For example, the UK Quality Assurance Agency for Higher Education defines personal development planning (PDP) as 'a structured and supported process undertaken by an individual to reflect upon their own learning, performance and/or achievement and to plan for their personal, educational and career development'. Clearly, a very wide range of activities and associated information could exist under this banner of PDP.

In an attempt to classify portfolio information in a way that relates usefully to PDP practice, Helen Richardson and I surveyed the current practice in 2002 to 2003 and came up with a list of information that was likely to appear in (largely paper-based) PDP activities. The list primarily contained such information as was already well used in practice, but we also added a few other categories of information that seemed likely for the future, as we wanted the list to cover anything that was likely to be suggested by PDP practitioners.

The full list is included as an appendix to this book, alongside the associated list of PDP activities that we found. The list of information types includes things normally found on CVs, personal situation statements, reflections (including on learning and performance), logs, goals and action plans, resources, support, and various other (less used) general and administrative information. If one extrapolates beyond past and current practice, there are few limits as to what might count as personal development when undertaken by individuals themselves.

As we trace through historical practice, it is notable how what starts off as a well-defined set of information for assessment develops, through rational steps, towards covering just about anything in which the individual is interested. The temptation in the end is to regard the e-portfolio simply as a container for any materials of interest to the individual, or for presentation to others. While this is plausible, throwing everything into one large bucket loses much of the real meaning and structure inherent in the information, and we do better to avoid that.

Information relevant to purposes

An alternative to understanding portfolio information on the basis of past and current practice is to mirror the above discussion of purpose. There, the primary distinction was made between information used for our own purposes, and that used in connection with other people.

Information used primarily for our own purposes is naturally connected with reflection. For example, diaries, logs and journals fall within this category. The structure of the information contained in these is fairly straightforward: in addition to the text that forms the content of the entry, there is also a date when it was written, and possibly a date when it was last revised, and, conceivably, reference to one or more other dates. Records for reflection may be simply records of what your experiences were during a certain period of time, but they may also be structured. You might write something in response to structured questions about the experiences you have chosen to record. For example, you might ask about a particular aspect of those experiences, or write with the intention of reflecting on them with a particular objective in mind. While different approaches to personal and professional development may focus on the different aspects of the experiences, no scheme can be applied to *every* piece of reflective writing.

To express feelings or emphasise certain aspects to aid later reflection, plain text can be embellished in a number of ways. For example, embellishments might be typographical in nature, such as font size, colour and style. Expressions may also be of a different kind, such as pictures, photographs, diagrams, voice recordings or videos.

Reflective writing may also be related to other things of interest. It can, for example, relate to something that happened, something that is in progress, or something that is aimed for or achieved. Any piece of writing can also be related to other pieces of writing. It can be one of a set; it can follow on from another piece; it can be a revision of a previous piece. All these relationships, as well as the reflective writing itself, can potentially be represented in an e-portfolio system.

Beyond your own purposes, the other main category was purposes that focus on other people; generally this involves other people reading the material, at some point. Social convention applies more to interactions between people than to private thought, and so information for reading by others tends to be more structured – or even more formal. One common theme is that your audience is looking for evidence of your abilities or particular characteristics. Even if they are just trying to sense what kind of person you are, they will have certain things they are looking for, related to the ways they think they can assess or evaluate you. To communicate well with your audience, you must arrange your information following the structures they are looking for.

We are familiar with the kinds of things that typically and traditionally make their way into CVs, for use in the worlds of education and employment. These tend to comprise experiences (in education and work), knowledge, abilities, qualifications, courses taken, results of assessments (e.g. of knowledge, ability, attainment, etc.), aspirations, and perhaps also leisure interests.

Simply listing your abilities or characteristics is barely evidence. You might list qualifications and the results of other assessments, but an e-portfolio offers wide-ranging possibilities for providing evidence, or at least pointers to evidence, beyond such lists. All sorts of things that can be represented digitally might conceivably be used as evidence of something of interest to someone else. Thus, portfolio information needs to be able to include those digital artefacts, as well as a way of linking those artefacts to the abilities or characteristics that they demonstrate.

I will not try to list the different sorts of things that might serve as evidence – to include everything you might think of, the list would be enormous. We may as well start afresh, considering all the kinds of things that could be in a portfolio.

The inherent nature of portfolio information

A third way to consider portfolio information is by taking a very general look at the structure of the information itself, and the philosophical concepts related to that information. A word of caution before we start on that: the structure of any information, like all organisation and categorisation, is something which comes across to different people in different ways. As such, the following discussion is necessarily a personal view – philosophical, but I hope also practical.

To start with, I want to set out a view of the world of which portfolios are a part. In this view of the world, there are four fundamental kinds of things:

- First, there is what is out in the world already. This includes, on the one hand, things of the natural world, and things that have been made by people. These exist independent of any particular description, and have a continuing identity across time. On the other hand, there are also events and occasions that happen in time, involving physical things: lessons, holidays, jobs, courses, visits to a pub or a football match, a football match itself, passing a driving test, winning a race, being awarded a knighthood, and countless other such things. We could call all of this 'the material world', with the term being understood to refer to things which have materialised, rather than which are still expected to come. The term 'real world' is too broad: the worlds of thought and communication are also real, although the term 'realised' might be closer to the intention here.

- Second, there is a particularly important subset of the abovementioned 'material world', namely agents – people and organisations – who are capable of doing things intentionally, and who therefore can be legally responsible. These agents are the central players in social and political reality.
- Third, there are general concepts or patterns, which are repeatable, rather than being fixed to particular things or events. Concepts serve as labels, to talk about or classify particular things or events. Relevant examples of these are skills, and topics of interest. We could identify this as the world of thought.
- Fourth, there are records or expressions, whether written, spoken or acted. These include books, notes, poems, plays, films, questions or answers. (This does not mean a physical thing like a particular copy of a book, but rather the record or expression which might be embodied in any number of physical copies of the book etc.) These 'records' typically refer to other kinds of thing. They might refer to particular things, events or occasions in the material world, to general concepts in the world of thought, or to other records. This includes what one might otherwise call 'information' about other things. We could call this the world of record and communication.

This very general set of distinctions does not pretend to be advanced philosophy or even best classifying practice, and many questions could be raised about it. But philosophical nicety is not the point; rather we want something here that is meaningful in practical and commonsense terms. The significance is that for portfolio purposes, these divisions provide the basis for categories that are easy to understand and to use for practical classification, without worrying about the inevitably complex borderline cases.

As a philosophical aside, the material world of the first and second groups of things tends to have so-called 'extensional' definitions, while the world of thought in the third group of things tend to have 'intensional' (with an 's', not a second 't') definitions. Definitions, as forms of words, themselves belong to the fourth group, of expressions or records.

With these four important kinds of things in mind, we can turn back to considering how to classify e-portfolio information. The most important point to note at the outset is that an e-portfolio just contains information, and nothing in an e-portfolio belongs immediately to the embodied world of reality. Everything is just a record or an expression, but those records or expressions tend to be about things in the world. So when we are considering e-portfolio information, we are not thinking of the actual objects or agents or events in the material world, but expressions about or records about them; not the concepts of the world of thought, but definitions of or relations between those concepts.

Because portfolios are used to record information, it makes little sense to use the above four-point definition for portfolio information, as only one of the four categories is for records. Rather, we need to translate between the abovementioned four categories of things in the world as they relate to portfolios, and the four categories of items actually found in portfolios, which will be explained next. These categories of portfolio information are still rather abstract and general, but please bear with me, and I hope you will shortly see how they relate to the items that we are familiar with in portfolios.

Records or expressions in themselves

Typically, a record or expression is a piece of writing. There are many other possibilities, but writing is the most obvious one to consider, as it is very common in e-portfolios, and illustrates important issues. A piece of writing has its own internal history: it was composed over some time, perhaps published or issued at a certain time, and may have been revised at times. It has one or more authors. It can probably be summarised (though it may not have been). Much the same can be said of other media and modes of expression.

A useful point of reference for this is the increasingly widespread practice of blog writing. A blog entry is essentially an expression or record. With early, simple blog systems, all that one could do was to write, and the only way of organising blog entries was chronologically. It is this original view of blogs that corresponds most closely to the present view of expressions in themselves. Because a blog could be about anything at all, or nothing, the technical representation of blogs covered just the expression in itself, the date of creation, revision, and perhaps a few other details, all of which are reflected in the current specifications for communicating blog entries and 'feeds', that is, collections of entries.

'Expressions' as a term is a little safer than 'records', because the idea of a record can refer to the material objects that embody the expressions, and that is not intended here. It is important to note that while records or expressions in this sense do not refer directly to anything in the material world, a certain material piece of paper can exhibit the pattern of a particular expression.

Records of, or expressions about, particular agents and things of, or events in, the material world

Using the terms 'record' and 'expression' in their natural senses, a portfolio record might typically be seen as concerning something or someone, while an expression tends to concern a particular subject.

An important class of records would concern one particular object, person, agent or event from the material world, as in the first two kinds of things in the abovementioned philosophical view. A piece of writing in your portfolio could be about a person – you perhaps – in which case it might, for instance, be called a personal statement. Or it could be about someone else – as happens in a testimonial or reference – or it could be about an organisation. On the other hand, the writing could be about something that has happened – an event or an occasion. This is such a typical class of things to write about in portfolios that good examples pop up immediately in the imagination: descriptions of jobs, courses, achievements, etc. Indeed, a large proportion of portfolio writings are this kind of expression about particular things of the material world, whether objects, agents or events.

The particular thing being written about could also be a compound subject – as writing about a particular country might involve much writing about parts or aspects of that country.

Records about general patterns or concepts

A piece of writing could be about a pattern or concept, although writing in portfolios about patterns is perhaps most typically done through writing about the things or events which embody those patterns. Writing about a concept, without focusing on related things or events (except as examples) is more likely to be found in definitions, encyclopaedia articles, and more generally in academic papers.

In portfolio practice, it has always been useful to relate particular records to abilities, such as knowledge, skills, attitudes, personal qualities or other attributes. Abilities are by nature concepts rather than parts of the material world, and because concepts are (in this view) quite different from material things, it is not surprising that representing abilities in portfolios has been a challenge.

For certain abilities there are widely recognised definitions. One good example in the vocational domain is the UK's set of National Occupational Standards, managed by the UK's Sector Skills Councils. In the educational domain, there are many frameworks of skills, learning objectives, and outcomes, and a very substantial part of portfolio technology relates to the provision and management of evidence for whether individuals have the skills defined in such frameworks.

Relationships between these expressions

People (written about in one kind of portfolio record) write all kinds of portfolio records and expressions: as authors, they are taking responsibility for recording the records and expressing the expressions. People and organisations have rights – of ownership, intellectual property or whatever – over records and over things. Patterns are seen in particular things in the real world. For instance, an interest, which can be seen more as a concept than something tangible, relates to those activities, achievements and goals that are relevant to it.

The relationship between portfolio holders and their abilities is quite special. You may, for example, want to claim that you have a particular ability; equally you may want to mention an ability that you are trying to master, but do not yet claim. As such, if you want to claim an ability, you will need to be clear that you are claiming it, not just seeking it.

These are just some first examples to give a general idea of relationships within portfolio information. The following discussion will describe other relationships between the different kinds of information emerging from the three approaches detailed above.

Kinds of information that are relevant to e-portfolios

That was a rather detailed look at the inherent nature of portfolio information. Having considered the three treatments of the nature of portfolio information, we are now in a position to consider the individual kinds of information from the broader viewpoint of a synopsis of those three treatments, rather than just basing our categories on one approach.

Information about the portfolio holder and other agents

For any portfolio, there is a need to identify who it concerns – in other words, to define the portfolio holder. At a most basic level, when a portfolio is used in conjunction with an institutional information system, identification might be done simply through the holder's ID, as all other details could be supplied from the institutional informational system. However, for a portfolio system to convey who the portfolios are about, to other people, it needs information such as name and contact details; these could come from another information system, or be entered by the holder.

Other information about the portfolio holder that is commonly wanted in portfolio presentations is the kind of personal detail that is found in CVs. As these are familiar to most people of working age, no more need be said here.

In any portfolio, it might be appropriate to refer to other individuals and organisations ('agents' in terms of the philosophical analysis above). While it is possible to record the details of these other agents along with the job, the project, or whatever they are associated with, it is more efficient to record just once the relevant information about them, and then to link back to this record where appropriate; this will also reduce the likelihood of errors. In an individual portfolio, the information about other people will naturally be less extensive than the information about yourself, the holder. We can also imagine team portfolios where several people have equal treatment.

The more stable the personal information, and the more often it is to be reused, the more useful it is to record it in a portfolio for practical reuse. If information is likely to be used only once, such as replies to 'why are you interested in this particular job?', it is less important to record it for reuse.

Artefacts and other resources that could serve as evidence

You might want your portfolio to include or refer to things you have written or made, as evidence of your abilities and of what kind of person (or artist, or writer, etc.) you are. This is central to any assessment of you, but also useful for your own reflective awareness of what you can do. A piece of coursework, as in the example of Avril in Chapter 2, serves as a good example of this kind of portfolio information.

Alongside the things that you have made yourself (or collaborated in making), there are things that you find useful, or have found useful. There is no necessary difference in kind between things made by you and things made by others. What differences there are relate to what is known as the 'metadata' – the information about those things – such as the identity of their creator, author, owner or person responsible.

The information associated with digital resources is highly variable. If you examine the properties of any file on your computer, you may see several fields of associated information. But which fields are actually filled in, and whether they are accurate, varies greatly. Digital photo files, for example, often include associated information identifying the camera model, date and time taken, etc. But for documents, I have often seen files where, for example, the author field has been brought over from a previous document unchanged. As such, we cannot rely on this associated information without checking it. We also need to allow for files with no associated information, so we are generally better off recording such associated information as part of the information stored explicitly in the portfolio system, rather than leaving it only in the file itself. This has the added advantage that, for portfolio purposes, we can add extra information which may not be possible to represent in the files themselves.

Resources and associated information can appear in different ways in an e-portfolio system. First, you can include a digital resource in a portfolio, and include any associated information, or write about it in a separate portfolio entry. Similarly, you can link to a digital resource that is available on the web, but still record information associated with the resource in the portfolio system.

Second, you can describe individual resources, including non-digital ones, that you cannot or do not include or link to digitally. Such resources may themselves be particular parts of the material world – a car, say, or a sculpture – or they may themselves be expressions, such as books, articles or notes. People and organisations can be seen as resources as well. A course of education that you might undertake may have been a potentially significant resource to you, so why not describe that as well?

Third, you can list resources, whether they are physical, digital or a mixture. The list would be treated as a record, that is, a piece of writing.

We can group together all these ways of recording artefacts, products and resources, not because they all share the same nature (they don't), but because it is impractical to draw dividing lines between different groups of things. They all refer to things you made, things you contributed to, or things that have been or might be useful.

Reflective writing and other expressions, assertions and claims

Reflective writing has several connections with portfolios. First, there are commentaries about your own work; these may reflect on a number of aspects of the work and are written to be read by others. Second, there is the writing that goes on within PDP and continuing professional development (CPD), aimed, quite possibly, at increasing your reflective abilities, as well as providing source material for learning about yourself. Third, although not necessarily reflective, many portfolio systems have the capability for some kind of electronic communication between users, and any e-mail message, or blog post used as communication, is essentially an expression, in terms of the earlier discussion.

Taking the philosophical view, material things are related to concepts and patterns through records and expressions of a particular character: those that are assertions or claims, which can be agreed with or disagreed with. A piece of poetry is also an expression, but it is hard to disagree with; perhaps it is even harder to disagree with a piece of music. Dislike in both cases is obviously possible, but this is quite separate from disagreement. In contrast, it should be possible to disagree with an expression designed as a claim or assertion: there should be the possibility of evidence confirming or denying its truth. Some of the supporting evidence may typically be given or pointed to in the portfolio including that claim.

Expressions, assertions and claims do not necessarily describe anything, and are not in their essence descriptions, but rather they are themselves (although they may happen to describe something). Their function in relation to the rest of the world is by pointing to the connections in the world, rather than to mere existence, which is covered by the other kinds of portfolio information.

Some PDP or CPD practice typically revolves around the construction or writing of these assertions and claims.

As has been set out above, records of this kind of information do not have much common structure beyond what relates to any piece of writing, such as a blog entry.

Achievements and goals

This type of information moves beyond the concept of the portfolio as a set of assessed artefacts and reflections, by adding just one vital piece of associated information, namely, a date of achievement, or a target date for goals. The date is added because it is a central part of the meaning of those records, enabling a chronological view of progress in a person's life. For a goal, it represents the date by which it is planned to have reached the goal, and it is very useful to have this in machine-processable form, so that, for example, reminders can be sent. For a completed achievement (including qualifications gained), this date represents the date on which the achievement was actually achieved, and can be used by a portfolio system in presenting achievements together in some kind of chronological order.

Achievements in general may be just stated, or self-certified, or certified by another person or an authority. What distinguishes a qualification from other achievements is that it has the backing of a recognised award-giving body. It should also, like some other educational achievements, refer to a published curriculum or programme of experience, study or task, and assessment scheme.

Achievements and goals clearly belong to CVs, and to the PDP practice related to CVs, as well as to CPD.

Action plans represent another area of information associated with goals. Project plans have this sort of information, and project planning tools allow you to break down a goal into sub-goals and planned activities. This strong connection can be turned on its head, so that in some people's view, it is the plan that is central, while the goal appears as just one aspect of the plan to achieve it. Whichever of the two ends you count as more significant, the same relationships exist between goals, sub-goals and the actions planned to fulfil them. Sub-goals can be seen as contributing to or supporting their higher-level goal, and actions can be seen as supporting the sub-goal they contribute towards most directly.

In terms of the philosophical categories discussed above, an achievement is a part of the material world, in that it is tied to particular happenings in time and space. A goal is slightly different. Because a goal remains to be achieved, it is not yet a part of the material world, but only a projection or prediction, based on the pattern or patterns which are held as goals. An achievement which fulfils the goal shares the same pattern as that goal, but is definitely a part of the material world.

Goals and achievements only make sense in terms of intentional action by agents. This implies a relationship between the agents and their goals or achievements. The relationship between a portfolio holder and an achievement is fairly straightforward: the holder was completely, or partly, or not, responsible for the achievement happening. But for goals it is slightly different. Goals can be given up, put aside, rejected and no longer acted on. There is no material relationship between goals and agents, as that relationship still belongs to the world of thought. The expression of a goal is a bit like a claim, whose author or creator is the person who takes responsibility for it, at least in e-portfolio systems that are built around the assumption of being controlled by their holder. Because goals are inherently revisable, portfolio holders may or may not want to record past goals that have been abandoned.

Activities and experiences

Unlike achievements and goals, which require just one date, namely the target or achievement date, representing activities and experiences requires two dates – a start and end date.

Activities and experiences are a classic part of CVs, representing, in particular, employment and courses undertaken. From a PDP perspective, meetings fall under the same heading. Meetings can play a highly significant role in PDP, because they play a part in the formulation and monitoring of goals, plans, actions and achievements.

Significant events are those with which the portfolio holder is presently engaged, as well as those in which the portfolio holder has actually participated – a material fact. In addition, portfolio information may include things that are planned to happen. But as with the difference between achievements and goals, so there is a difference between future events and those in the past and present. For example, the portfolio holder can start by considering whether to participate in an activity; move on to planning it firmly, and then eventually start it. An activity can be underway, and if things go to plan, it can be completed. Of course, not all activities that are started are also finished, and for reflection it may be useful also to represent activities that have been abandoned after their start, or rejected as options even before they were started.

Abilities and other patterns and concepts

As mentioned previously, skills and other abilities and qualities are important in portfolios generally. In traditional artists' portfolios, the nature and evidence of the artist's abilities may be implicit in the artefacts. In contrast, in skills-oriented CVs the idea is to make the nature of what is claimed quite explicit, and probably to provide, or at least point to, some kind of evidence for these skills.

At the risk of repetition, it is worth emphasising that within a portfolio, abilities need to be recorded as impersonal patterns that different people can display at different times and in different situations. To work effectively in information terms, an ability needs to be defined somewhere, ideally somewhere public, not inside an individual portfolio. The portfolio holder then has a number of possibilities.

You can 'tag' activities and achievements as being associated with the pattern of the ability. This gives you a set of things to review when reflecting on the extent to which you have that ability. If you think your ability comes up to a particular standard, or even if you just think it is worth saying something definite about, you can make a claim to that effect, and back up this claim with what evidence you may have.

But claiming an ability is not the only relationship you can have with it. Particularly in the action planning aspect of PDP, you can be aiming to acquire an ability. The goal is for you, in your capacity as a learner, to be able to exhibit the pattern as defined by the definition of the ability. If you achieve this, you can claim that you do now exhibit this pattern.

Alongside skills, although with less emphasis, in CVs we also tend to see interests. The general view seems to be that recording interests helps to show what kind of person you are, and perhaps gives a lead on some of your personal values (which will be discussed in Part 3). Perhaps also, recording interests as motivating factors gives an employer, or a colleague, a handle on how to motivate you in a work context. In any case, because interests are of somewhat lesser importance in the context of employment, they tend not to have been clearly defined, and so there is a greater onus on the portfolio holder to write a description of whatever interests he or she may have.

Another kind of pattern that may be relevant to portfolios has recently been identified more clearly. People adapt their behaviour to different kinds of situation, and those kinds of situation, along with people's behaviour, tend to fall into a number of distinct patterns. In *Multiplicity: The New Science of Personality*, Rita Carter calls these patterns 'personalities', and she suggests a definition of a personality in her sense as 'a coherent and characteristic way of seeing, thinking, feeling, and behaving'. This is important to the presentation of oneself through portfolios, because it is only possible to present coherently one personality at a time. If one tries to mix more together, the whole may well appear incoherent and inconsistent. This issue will be revisited in Part 3 of this book. For the moment, it is sufficient to say that personality, in this sense, seems to fit in as a kind of pattern, even if it differs from the other kinds of pattern.

CVs, action plans and other composite objects

CVs and action plans are both essentially composed of a number of parts. It is helpful to group them together on that basis, together with anything else that is essentially a selection or collection. In both CVs and action plans, one might expect short 'clips' of the information that makes up the selections, which in an e-portfolio may link to fuller versions.

These are all the types of portfolio items that I will distinguish here. The other kind of portfolio information is the relationship between items, of which there are many kinds, but we will look at just one example.

One particular relationship: evidence

There are many possible relationships between items of portfolio information, and it is not intended to make a list of them here. But one is particularly significant: the relationship of one thing being evidence of another.

Portfolio holders want to make claims, whether implicit or explicit, about their history, their experience, their achievements and their abilities. Those claims are to be substantiated through evidence, and this evidence is vital to give confidence to the reader that the portfolio is not a work of fiction.

The kind of material which can be used as evidence is very varied. Simply writing at length about something offers the evidence of a coherent story, in that it is much easier maintaining coherence about something that is true than about something which is invented. Writing itself, if genuinely by the portfolio holder, can be evidence of writing ability, and may be taken as evidence of knowledge.

If you record that one thing in your portfolio is evidence of another thing in your portfolio, what you have recorded is not, in itself, evidence, but rather it is an indication of what you believe should be taken as evidence. What you are saying is that A tends to imply B; if someone believes (or verifies) A, then they should have a stronger belief in B. You may thus record that you believe one of your achievements is good evidence of one of your abilities. You may also suggest that the fact that you undertook an activity successfully should be taken as evidence of an ability. However, the records of these things, in themselves, do not constitute hard evidence, as the records could have been invented.

Harder evidence is discussed in the following chapter under the heading of authentication and verification.

Other aspects of portfolio information

Other aspects of portfolio information have been helpful to some people's understanding in the past, and so may be worth setting out here.

The first aspect is the relationship between the predictability of use of the portfolio information and the tightness of the specification of what should be in the portfolio. Some uses of e-portfolio information are highly predictable. The most exemplary case here is for assessment portfolios, where the particular selection of information gathered is used in a formalised way, probably just once. Other uses are much less predictable. If one writes a diary, or a log, or tags certain information as relevant to certain topics, it may not be at all clear how and when this information is going to be reused. Tight, predictable use of the information tends to go along with very clear specification of what is required, what format it is to follow, and how it is to be presented. The less predictable the information reuse, the less likely that one optimal format can be clearly defined.

A second aspect of portfolio information is whether it is intended only for direct reading by people, or also for use by systems in the course of their operation. Complex explanations are always just meant for reading by people. To help future searches, it might be possible to index the words used in the explanation; in addition, the most sophisticated systems can search the explanations for word patterns that correspond to concepts. However, there is not much more that can be done automatically with a complex piece of text. If we do want to allow more automatic functionality, we need to introduce clearly structured data. Above, we have already discussed dates, which are very useful to enable a system to display items in chronological order, or for making queries for information relating to particular periods of time. And although adding more structured information may look like the same kind of approach as is taken for assessment, in reality it is just the opposite. One set of very commonly used structured information about records is called Dublin Core. Because Dublin Core is so widely known, if you associate Dublin Core metadata with your record, the information stands a good chance of being recognised in any application that deals with Dublin Core. The end result is that, rather than restricting your information to one single use, you will have opened it up to automatic uses that you had not anticipated, the first of which is more accurate and targeted search.

As we will see later, these issues have an impact on the interoperability of portfolio tools.

References and further reading

Rita Carter's *Multiplicity: The New Science of Personality* (2008).

The IMS Global Learning Consortium website (*http://www.imsglobal.org/*) contains further information on the IMS Learner Information Package specification (see *http://www.imsglobal.org/profiles/*).

The UK's National Occupational Standards are produced by Sector Skills Councils (and some other bodies), which are supervised by the UK Commission for Employment and Skills (*http://www.ukces.org.uk/*).

The Dublin Core definitions are managed by the Dublin Core Metadata Initiative (*http://dublincore.org/*).

The UK Quality Assurance Agency for Higher Education defines PDP on its website (see *http://www.qaa.ac.uk/academicinfrastructure/progressfiles/archive/policystatement/default.asp#pdp*).

7

Issues with portfolio information

Nothing in this book constitutes legal advice. Consult a lawyer for any desired or necessary legal opinion or assistance.

Data protection outline

Data protection considerations need to underpin all work with other people's personal information.

As we have discussed previously, many different people have some interest in information about individuals. The law in the UK in general is that bodies can only hold personal information for legitimate purposes, for which they are either explicitly registered or for which they are exempted from the provisions of the relevant acts. Bodies are not allowed to pass on personal information to other bodies without legitimate authorisation to do so. Particular care is required for what is defined as 'sensitive' personal information (e.g. mental and physical health, religious affiliation and beliefs, ethnicity).

Exemptions to the UK Data Protection Act 1998 are given in its Part IV. One exemption that might be considered for some portfolio purposes, is Section 36, and is short enough to quote in full: 'Personal data processed by an individual only for the purposes of that individual's personal, family or household affairs (including recreational purposes) are exempt from the data protection principles and the provisions of Parts II and III'. It is conceivable that Section 36 might cover personal development planning in some settings, but whether it does or not would be a matter for a lawyer's advice.

The situation with the learner- or user-centred kind of portfolio systems is generally that the portfolio holders enter the information themselves. They are implicitly but clearly asking for it to be stored. However, they do not automatically give permission for any other use of that information. Those in charge of portfolio systems need to take great care that the information recorded by users is not made available to anyone else, or for any other purpose, in any form which allows identification of individuals, except as specifically allowed by the portfolio holder (or otherwise by law) (see the Joint Information Systems Committee's Code of Practice, in the chapter references). The issues here are broadly similar to those arising from the storage of personal information in other contexts. It may well be best, not only to set out clear policies about exactly what is going to happen to any information entered (including how long it will be held for), but also to ensure that those policies continue to be understood by the users of the system. This procedure is even more vital where the portfolio system is designed to play a part in a formal process such as assessment, which may be public.

In addition to what organisations do with personal information, particularly in educational institutions, there is also the question of how to educate people to be responsible about their own personal information as well as that of other people. Giving people a long list of rules and advice when they register with the institution, or sign up to use the system, is really not sufficient. In particular, portfolio holders need to be made aware of the consequences of information about themselves being made public, whether on their own websites, through portfolio systems, through social networking services, or by someone else. This is very much a question that needs attention now and in the near future, and up to now I have not seen any treatments in any great depth.

There are many other legal issues surrounding portfolio systems and practice, and many of these have been detailed in reports commissioned by the Joint Information Systems Committee (JISC). Some such reports are given in the further reading section at the end of the chapter.

Authentication and verification

As mentioned under the earlier heading of 'evidence', it might be useful to be able to provide some assurance that e-portfolio information is genuine or true for people who view it.

There is a large volume of technical work on this issue that stands in its own right. As it has a much wider scope than e-portfolios and e-portfolio systems, I will treat it only as a marginal note to the main topics of this book.

Two broad kinds of technical approach to this issue can be distinguished, mirroring two traditional approaches to the same issue for paper documentation. On paper documentation, we see at least two different kinds of attempts to convey authority. The first is by signature, seal or similar device which is presumed to be difficult to forge, or where tampering may be obvious. Watermarks are used in banknotes, and often in certificates, on which it can state that they are only valid if they are printed on paper with that specific watermark. The second is to give the details of some authority with whom the information can be checked, or who is relied upon to provide true information. The electronic equivalents of both of these approaches are plausible and have been suggested, and in some cases tried out.

Anyone can copy a picture of a signature, so adding the image of a signature to an electronic document does little for security except to mean that any deception becomes a criminal forgery. Instead, digital signatures now mostly rely on a public key infrastructure (PKI), the discussion of which is far beyond the scope of this book. For our purposes, it is sufficient to say that documents can be digitally signed so that any tampering with them is evident. If someone changes the content of the document, it will clearly show that it is not in its original form when checked against the original signature. The issue remains, however, of establishing who digitally signed the document: how is that authority's identity verified?

The second broad kind of approach is to refer to a trusted source. This divides into two cases. First, taking the source of the document as a whole, you can look at where it comes from; this is also known as its provenance. If it comes from a reliable source, then it is more likely to be reliable.

The second case is to allow the information to be checked with a trusted source. The simplest way of doing this would be, as often with paper documentation, to provide the contact details of an authority who can verify the information. This neither deals with the problem of knowing whether the supposed authority is genuine, nor does it use technology in any new way. A way better matched to the nature of e-portfolios is to provide a link in the portfolio to substantially the same information held within the domain of the validating authority. So, for instance, I could claim that I had an 'A'-Level in mathematics, and the awarding body could have a public record with the date that Simon Grant passed 'A'-Level in mathematics; I could then include a link to that information in my portfolio. Unfortunately, awarding bodies do not yet provide this facility, but there seem no great obstacles in the way of doing it, for information that is in the public domain. If the information is private in any way, then I would need to give a reader permission, for which I might have a password to give out, and the technical implementation would be more complex, although well within what is routinely done at present in different contexts.

This won't be discussed here further. For further reading, see the list at the end of the chapter.

Information interoperability

As soon as information is represented in a way that is more structured than just plain text, there arises the issue of whether or not that representation is compatible with the representations that other systems would use in representing the same information. (In fact, this used to be the case even with plain text, but fortunately first ASCII and now Unicode and UTF have made things much easier.) Human nature seems to be such that different people will usually represent things differently, without any particularly principled reason, based just on the differences between the ways that different people see the world. If different people have designed different e-portfolio systems without reference to any common standard or guidance, it is likely that the information they represent will not be wholly compatible. In this situation, the job of an interoperability specification is to provide the best basis for each system to map the information to, so that the maximum amount of information can be transferred meaningfully between systems.

Why be interoperable in this way? There are just a few general scenarios that keep recurring in discussions. The first and maybe simplest scenario is for backing up information and restoring it to the same system, or another system using the same software. It is not trivial to save information from a database in a form that is both human-readable and that can also be restored into the same system. But if this is the only requirement, systems can do this for themselves and do not need interoperability with any other systems.

The second general scenario is when a portfolio system user transfers from one institution to another, and the two institutions do not have the same portfolio systems. There is potential value in being able to transfer at least some of the portfolio information that has been built up, so that processes in the new institution can use or refer to information that has been gathered in the old institution. This is not yet something which is required every day, for several reasons. Personal development planning (PDP) processes will need to be more widespread, and share more common ground, before people will be able to transfer information routinely from one system to another. This should change in the coming few years. Another reason is that, at present, comparatively few learners put a great deal of time into creating their portfolios: if the information were lost, it would be relatively straightforward to re-enter. However, this could be a kind of self-fulfilling prophecy: if the interoperability does not exist, learners will not have any sense of security that the work they do on one system will live longer, and therefore they might not be motivated in the first place to create records worth transferring. And if there are no records worth transferring, there is little motivation for developing interoperability. As such, providing interoperability is a very good idea in any case, and could turn the self-fulfilling prophecy the other way.

The third general scenario is where different systems are working at the same time in parallel, perhaps storing different parts of your information. This may happen if you are studying in more than one institution at once, or if you are studying while working. If the information stored on different systems is about different things, you may want to access the information on the other system, rather than the one being used presently. If the same information is stored in different places, then when information is updated on one, it also needs to be sent to the other(s) for update. This scenario could apply, for instance, to the interaction between a dedicated e-portfolio system, and a student record system of the type that exists in many institutions, holding personal details and official records, many of which might be useful in a portfolio or PDP context.

A very brief and technical history

Portfolio tools are sufficiently new that there was no agreed interoperability specification before 2001. At that point there were two 'competing' specifications for 'learner information': 'PAPI Learner', developed under the IEEE, and the Learner Information Package (LIP) developed by IMS. Both had problems, and neither attracted a substantial implementation base, although PAPI Learner was quickly marginalised.

The IMS ePortfolio specification was published in 2005, and built several missing features on top of IMS LIP. Around the same time, BSI British Standards commissioned a UK version of IMS LIP, UKLeaP, which developed in parallel with IMS ePortfolio. However, it too was closely tied to IMS LIP, and has subsequently been abandoned.

Together, IMS ePortfolio and UKLeaP gave a reasonable idea of the kind of information that practitioners and developers thought would be useful to be able to communicate for e-portfolio interoperability. This covers much of the ground detailed above. IMS ePortfolio added structures for 'presentation' and 'view', covering the use of e-portfolios as presentations.

The only area of e-portfolio use which these specifications do not cover so well is assessment, where the information required is tightly focused on specific sets of skills, abilities or competences, and the certification of learners' attainment of them.

Meanwhile, the HR-XML consortium has been continually developing specifications for the exchange of human resources-related data, and this overlaps significantly with e-portfolio information. At the time of writing, this is being developed from HR-XML 2.5, which is also a very complex set of specifications, to HR-XML 3.0, which will not be backwards-compatible with HR-XML 2.5, but will introduce a degree of rationalisation and modularisation.

In December 2006, in response to the lack of any effective and straightforward standard or specification, a JISC CETIS special interest group began to develop a simpler and more practical UK-originated specification. To indicate going beyond UKLeaP, and to connect with the then recent 'Web 2.0' concept, the name 'LEAP 2.0' was chosen. Alongside LEAP 2.0, in 2008 JISC funded some portfolio interoperability projects, which put together what the developers felt was a straightforward developer-friendly XML specification, based on the Atom Syndication Format, and called (at least temporarily) LEAP2A. This provides the main (but not necessarily the only) XML 'binding' of LEAP 2.0, simultaneously providing a solid basis for LEAP 2.0 in development practice, and drawing from the larger set of concepts that are still being brought together in LEAP 2.0 to underpin further development.

Current aspirations

The concepts behind LEAP 2.0 are subtle. Recognising that it is not a good idea simply to proliferate XML specifications, LEAP 2.0 refers back instead to the Semantic Web. In terms of the Semantic Web, the representation of any information is done in terms of a 'directed named graph', which in simple terms can be illustrated as many named 'blobs' with named 'arrows' connecting them. Each blob represents the focus of one instance of the previously described kinds of portfolio information. Each arrow represents a relationship between a 'blob' and another 'blob', or a value (a piece of text, number, date, etc.) which does not have its own 'blob'. A fundamental premise of the Semantic Web is that these 'blob and arrow' diagrams provide a common way for representing a vast range of kinds of information, including any information that is likely to be wanted in connection with e-portfolios. This approach to

Issues with portfolio information

representing information is so simple and powerful that I believe it is unlikely to be superseded in the near future.

The Atom-based approach of LEAP2A has been chosen to make the representation relatively easy to understand and to implement, and it is hoped that more and more systems will be able to implement interoperability functionality on that basis. LEAP2A will be mapped to the more general LEAP 2.0 RDF. It will also be possible to map other XML-based specifications onto LEAP 2.0, and thus provide some higher-level interoperability with LEAP2A.

The always important consideration about interoperability

It is always worth keeping in mind that effective interoperability between e-portfolio tools and systems depends vitally on identifying correspondences between the e-portfolio practice of the various institutions, and ensuring that what corresponds in practice is represented in compatible ways when the relevant information is given in the format used by the interoperability specifications. A mere conformance to a technical specification will not, by itself, ensure that e-portfolio information generated in one organisation can be reused in practice in another context or in another organisation.

Centralised and distributed storage of personal information

When the information to be stored for e-portfolio purposes, and its format, have been agreed, there is still the matter of how and where to store it. When building an e-portfolio system, there may be a presumption that the relevant information will all be stored in a single database to be accessed by the system, but this is by no means the only way of arranging things.

Your e-portfolio information may come to cover many years of your life, when you may have been attached to several different institutions of learning, employers or other organisations. The information relevant to a portfolio may be wholly or partly drawn from the records directly under your control, but may also be spread around different systems, each with their own regimes of security and permission.

The first approach to storage is to centralise it, with all the information being held on a single server. Once the information is there, it is relatively easy to hold and to present in a controlled way to other people who have accounts on the same server, and can be given specific permission to view particular portfolio information. To put this approach into practice, information that started on other systems must be moved or copied onto the central system. Potential problems include the information version control, which may be updated on one system and not another; and the loss of authoritativeness as information is copied away from its original source.

With the second approach, in contrast, storage is distributed across several servers or systems. This is a much more general case, and allows information to remain where it originated, or where it naturally belongs. However, the information may be more difficult to gather together, and it can be difficult to coordinate permissions across sites. If information is distributed in this way, there needs to be a way for one system to fetch information from another, which raises questions both of standardisation and of security.

Even in principle, the question is not easy to answer. What information should be kept by educational institutions, or by employers, on their own account, and what should be kept by the portfolio holders themselves? It would be fair to say that there is presently no clear consensus on this. In practice, yet more issues arise. Some information is so useful that it may be wanted in several different systems – contact information is the obvious example. What, then, is to be done to ensure consistency? And what if the holder is simultaneously working with several portfolio systems at once?

Starting from where the information is

A more practical concern than where the information should be stored is where it is actually stored now. Broadly speaking, student record systems store some general information which might be useful for a portfolio, such as names, contact details and nationality as well as such information as courses enrolled on and results achieved, possibly including grades, reports and other information entered by staff. Student record systems also store information that you probably wouldn't want in a portfolio, such as attendance records, fees paid, details of next of kin, religion, medical details, special needs, and possibly several other things. Somewhere in the administrative systems of an educational institution there may be everything that the institution might need to know about you, or might need to tell a government agency.

If information does not fall under this administrative category, it may be in what has been called the virtual learning environment (VLE), the learning management system (LMS), or the e-learning system of the institution. There one might find records of communications between staff and learners, or between learners; probably coursework submissions; and possibly feedback from tutors.

Employers' records are likely to vary vastly in scope. A small business employer may only keep personal details necessary for payroll and tax returns. A large employer may have an HR department with a comprehensive HR system, potentially including training records and training needs.

The information identified above as portfolio information is currently most likely to be held in a single institutional e-portfolio system, and it will be clear that there is scope for overlap with any other kinds of system.

Also potentially relevant to e-portfolios is the information that may be held by the learner on other systems outside the institution or organisation. Increasingly, many people use systems of their own choice for social networking, blogs, photographs, videos, employment search and application, dating, etc. The prospect of integrating all of these seems a long way off, but we will return to related ideas in Part 3.

The more limited question of integrating portfolio and administrative systems is covered further in Part 2.

References and further reading

Data protection, legal

The UK Data Protection Act 1998 is available online (*http://www.opsi.gov.uk/Acts/Acts1998/ukpga_19980029_en_1*).

The JISC's Code of Practice for the Further and Higher Education Sectors on the Data Protection Act 1998 is a very useful resource (*http://www.jisclegal.ac.uk/publications/DPACodeofPractice.htm*). At the time of writing, this was last updated in May 2008.

The JISC Legal and Records Management study web page (*http://www.jisc.ac.uk/whatwedo/programmes/buildmlehefe/learnerrecordslegalstudy.aspx*) contains resources that are less up to date, but still potentially useful.

Authentication, security

A useful short paper by a commercial company, Digitary, is referenced through the company's website (*http://www.digitary.net/digitary-paper-at-eunis-in-grenoble*).

A suitable book for starting to explore the subject in more depth is Philip J. Windley's *Digital Identity* (2005).

Interoperability

One of the major players in interoperability for the portfolio domain has been the IMS Global Learning Consortium (*http://www.imsglobal.org/*). In 2001 they produced the IMS Learner Information Package specification (*http://www.imsglobal.org/profiles/*), and then in 2005 the IMS ePortfolio specification (*http://www.imsglobal.org/ep/*).

The recent work done in conjunction with the JISC and JISC CETIS is currently documented at:

- *http://wiki.cetis.ac.uk/Portfolio_interoperability_projects*
- *http://wiki.cetis.ac.uk/LEAP_2.0*
- *http://wiki.cetis.ac.uk/LEAP2A_specification*

This may however change in the future. Searching for 'PIOP' and 'LEAP2A' may help find relevant pages.

8

The need for common terms in portfolio information

We have looked from several different perspectives at the information that portfolios are designed to record and communicate, and identified information about people, about what they have done, and what they can do. If you wrote something purely for personal reflection, you would hope to remember what you meant by writing it. But if information is to be communicated, it must use common terms in ways understandable by your audience, in a way very similar to the need for human communications to use a common natural language.

So what are the common terms that need to be understood for communicating portfolio information? It depends on the purpose of the information and the kind of information stored. For use with assessment, the information required will generally be defined clearly by whoever is doing the assessing. But for other uses, it may not initially be so clear.

Take a CV as an example. Some information is relatively clear, and we routinely share the terms used. Educational institutions and businesses have unique names, at least within a country. Less clearly, job titles can be much more misleading, and that gives one reason for stating just what kind of work was done in any significant job. When it comes to abilities, skills, competences or whatever you want to call them, things really start to get interesting, and possibly confusing.

The formal and official nature of qualifications has some advantages. At least for formal qualifications, there are usually reasonably clear definitions of the syllabus or programme of study, and of the assessment procedure. But for employment and employability, it has long been recognised that it has not been easy to capture many important aspects of employability in traditional qualifications, and that the skills or competences that go by such names as 'employability skills', 'key skills' or 'transferable skills' are important alongside formal qualifications. While there is broad general agreement about what different key skills are generally about, there is no such agreement on either precise definitions or methods of assessment.

For illustration, take the topic of working with others, or team working or group working. There is no consistency even in the term used. This is not something that has traditionally been assessed in the individual-centred assessment regimes of traditional qualifications: all that could be assessed through individual examinations would be knowledge about team work. Nonetheless, most employers recognise that productive employees have to be able to work with others in teams, and that some people are better at it than others.

How could team working (or any other such ability, skill or competence) be defined in a useful way that served all applications in education, e-portfolios, personal development planning (PDP) and continuing personal development (CPD)? As suggested previously, in the worlds of education and employment, abilities need to be a common reference point for learning objectives, for goals to achieve, for achievements to claim and refer to, and for pathways leading from one stage of life to another. It is not easy to fulfil all these at once, but that needs to be the aim. There is clearly work to do to achieve commonly agreed terms and definitions.

A sensible approach to this is to break the definition of the skill down into its component parts. Doing this has three benefits. First, it makes explicit what the components are, which is in itself a valuable part of a definition. Second, it has been observed that lower-level definitions are less contentious, and easier to agree on, than higher-level ones, although at present there do not appear to be any studies that confirm this. Third, agreeing on and listing the component parts allows different authorities to disagree more clearly and with less confusion about the meaning of their higher-level terms.

Consider, for instance, the example of LUSID, developed for the University of Liverpool under the name 'Liverpool University Student Interactive Database', and taken forward by the University of Oxford under a different name. LUSID uses 'teamwork' interchangeably with 'working with others', and provides a short definition to the effect that: 'Teamwork is about working effectively with other people to achieve a common purpose'. In LUSID, each general skills area has several leading questions attached; these ask about different ways in which the general skill area can be evidenced, which provides a convenient analysis of what the skill means in practice. When LUSID was built, it was expected that the different institutions using it might disagree on which questions are relevant to their local definition, and the following list is simply the default one, which could be changed. For a general self-audit, imagine

The need for common terms

each sentence here starting 'Are you confident you are able to...', or, for help with analysis of the skills involved in a particular experience or activity, 'Did you have to...':

- recognise other people's feelings when not necessarily clearly stated in language?
- work as a member of a team, taking your own area of responsibility?
- identify own strengths and weaknesses as a member of the group?
- recognise the strengths and weaknesses of other group members and how they best contribute to the task?
- contribute to the resolution of misunderstandings and conflicts among group members?
- make contributions to group discussion which are clear, constructive and relevant to the task?
- negotiate clearly understood goals with other members of the group?
- contribute to the realistic planning of group activity, recognising constraints and opportunities?
- keep to an agreed timetable/plan of responsibility?
- evaluate the effectiveness of the group process?
- evaluate the effectiveness of the group product?
- recognise and take into account other people's perspectives?

I mentioned above that breaking the skill into its component parts helped others to disagree more clearly. LUSID added an explanation to each question, which helped clarify further, though we didn't manage to give a short label to each question, which would have made referring to each question easier.

Once the skill has been broken down in this way, one can imagine, for instance, some people deciding that evaluation of the effectiveness of group process and product is not itself part of team work, but something higher. There are no absolutely right or wrong opinions here, as what is right may depend on the context of related portfolio processes. One would expect that, for communication skills, an appropriate range of questions to consider might well differ between, say, artisans and diplomats.

In contrast to the differences of practice and of opinion in higher education, the UK's Sector Skills Councils have defined a large number of 'National Occupational Standards' for which there is wide agreement. Among these standards, there are definitions, for many occupational areas, of exactly what someone has to demonstrate the ability to do, in order to meet that standard, and what underlying knowledge they are expected to have, to support the effective practice.

In academic contexts, it has not proved to be so easy to arrive at common definitions, probably for several reasons. The outcomes and objectives of academic programmes of study are not so easily condensed into things people ought to be able to do and know about, and even if attempts were made to characterise them in that way, the difficulty of assessing them might prevent their being useful. Then, academics like to do things in their own way. This means that definitions can easily be different for every different academic, and are very often different between different higher education institutions. More generally, educational institutions, like any institutions, give rise to an institutional way of thinking about the whole educational process. The institutional view will include a view of what knowledge, skills, competences, etc., are relevant to the educational process as a whole. Along with this 'skills framework' as it could be called, whether explicit or implicit, there will be a set of milestones or progress markers, which could be framed in terms of performance in end-of-year examinations, tests or reviews.

This general lack of common terms in the academic world has negative consequences in two ways. First, it interferes with different institutions comparing the progress of their learners towards what should be commonly defined outcomes, to enable comparison to be made between the effectiveness of institutions for any of a number of reasons. Second, it interferes with recruiters' attempts to differentiate between different candidates, based on their ability and performance on the things of common interest to employers.

Not all of the academic world is so disjointed, however. There are positive initiatives. Some academic departments are relating more closely to the professional bodies to which their graduates progress. Increasingly, these professional bodies are defining what an undergraduate education should provide, and course designers can then start to craft their educational objectives or learning outcomes to work towards those professional definitions. Academic initiatives to link learning outcomes with professional requirements have been noted by colleagues in areas including:

- engineering;
- nursing and midwifery;
- ICT engineering;
- psychology;

- MBA courses;
- medicine;
- architecture and the built environment.

The remaining challenge is that the outcomes defined by professional bodies can still be difficult to formalise and to assess – more difficult than the standards defined in the National Occupational Standards documentation, which are the basis of many vocational courses and assessments.

The need for these kinds of common standard definitions of ability at higher educational levels, as well as in vocational education, is increasingly clear. Learners are less and less tied exclusively to one educational institution, there is more learning happening in the workplace, and they need clear goals to work towards. Learners are increasingly putting together their own courses and qualifications, with modules potentially drawn from different institutions or learning providers. Learning, including higher-level learning, still needs to extend further across and along individual lives. All of this will be helped by having clearer common definitions of the abilities being sought and claimed. ICT will play a vital role in determining how well this works.

The positive and negative role of ICT for common terms and definitions

As our overall subject is electronic portfolios, our discussion here naturally focuses on the role of ICT. ICT offers great potential both for disseminating common definitions and for facilitating their effective use. Just proposing terms and definitions is not enough: there must be a way in which they can be shared and used. While ICT is a powerful tool for this, it is not always helpful. There is the danger that ICT can promote practices which hinder the effective sharing of common definitions. So in this section we will look at how ICT can play an effective part in the process, and also what might go wrong.

From an ICT point of view, the ideal situation might be for every definition of an ability, skill, competence, or whatever you call it, to have a uniform resource identifier (URI), which is also a URL, through which names and definitions in various languages may be retrieved. (There doesn't have to be an actual document at the URL: it can be a database-driven site, or there can be a redirect from the URL to the page with information.) Because different institutions, organisations or companies often like to define their own terms, there would also need to be information about equivalence between different definitions, also available in a standard way. Each domain could define, for each term, which other terms in other domains they accepted as equivalent, and also, perhaps, which other terms included their one, or were included by their one.

Portfolio (and other) systems could use the URI, along with a title (i.e. a few words used in lists, for links, etc.) to refer to the ability. In particular, any claim that a portfolio holder had a certain defined ability would have a reference to the URI of the ability claimed. The portfolio information could be matched against a course or job requirement that used the same URI reference. Exact matching of URIs would only work if different organisations used exactly the same URI, but it would be easy enough to extend matching, either by searching each definition for the equivalent URIs specified by the owners of that definition, and matching if both referred to each other, or by allowing a single ability claim to refer to a set of ability definitions in the same claim. Course or training outcomes could have references to ability definition URIs in the same way, as could course or job requirements. This would in principle allow people to map out pathways of one or more courses, thereby getting them from where they are to where they want to be.

However, several problems could interfere with this ICT-enabled ideal.

First, institutions and organisations that create ability definitions could persist both in creating their own, even where other existing definitions would serve, and in failing to link their definitions to other related ones. This would provide definitions, but they would be no more usable than at present, and only comparable through human reading and appreciation. This is hard to counteract while people are in relatively closed institutions and liable to 'groupthink'.

Second, the definitions created in this way by organisations may not be what individual people want. Dissatisfied people may try to define their own categories, with even less standardisation, and less comparison possible. This is related to the phenomenon known as 'folksonomy'. A folksonomic approach is basically what happens when people tag items like photos in Flickr, or bookmarks in del.icio.us, using short text labels, often one or two words, without an explicit definition, and without any attempt to relate their definitions to the definitions of others. This kind of tagging may, if done carefully, result in things being effectively grouped together for each individual user, but the tag labels used can very easily be misleading to other people. Different people mean different things by the same word; different people use different words for the same concept, idea or pattern. People use different dialects and languages. All of these factors mean that grouping things together across different users, based on the similarity of different users' informal tags, is only likely to be effective for general and imprecise purposes. If the person assigning the tags has not given them a definition, there is no way to check up on their intention beyond looking at the things tagged and working out from that what the tag might mean.

In principle, a solution to this would be to give people well-defined concepts to use as tags that cover at least most of the meanings they want to assign to the things they want to classify, and make sure that the tagging process is still easy, although it would be hard to make it quite as easy as doing a single word tag in Flickr. But where would those well-defined concepts come from, and who would keep them up to date? Perhaps a better option is to take concepts which are in use in a community where the communication is mediated electronically, and to persuade the community as a whole to use the concepts and maintain the definitions.

If I have clarified the problem a little, that is enough for here in Part 1. In Part 2, Chapter 19, we will consider practical steps towards doing these things in a more positive way.

References and further reading

LUSID was a web-based skills audit and development system at the University of Liverpool. Janet Strivens was the practitioner expert; I contributed some ideas on web implementation, and the conceptual information systems architecture. A paper describing the system is: Janet Strivens and Simon Grant (2000) 'Integrated web-based support for learning employability skills', available at: *http://www.ifets.info/journals/3_1/strivens.html*.

9

Portfolio functionality

At this point, I'm hoping that if you have read all of the preceding chapters, you will have a fair understanding of the purposes for which e-portfolios are used, and the information they may deal with. But the major reason for a tool is to enable you to do things – in this case with or using the information, as they are information tools – in support of the purposes that you want to further.

However, what you can do with a tool is not wholly dictated by the purposes by themselves, or the information by itself, or even purposes and information together. Rather, to understand functionality, we need to ask, in terms of the information, just how might tools facilitate:

- inputting, capturing, collecting or generating, then storing the information;
- managing, maintaining and elaborating the information;
- using, reusing, presenting and communicating the information.

There could be other possible approaches to categorising the functionality of e-portfolio tools, but this seems to be the most obvious.

Defining the functionality can help with devising an interoperability specification. This is because definitions of functionality face two ways. A function can be something that is required in an application context, as well as something that is supplied by a human or technical system. A function is something that people might want a system to do (which might be performed by an e-portfolio tool), and at the same time, how they might use the tool to go about doing it.

Input and storage functions

Capturing relevant information from system usage

This kind of automatic capture is like what happens with logging software, which can record, for example, how much time has been spent editing a particular file.

One of the gains from the use of information technology, more than other technology, is that records can be generated by the mere fact of using a tool. This is familiar to all web users, even if just through shopping sites, where we can view, for example, a list of the things we have recently looked at. Taking this kind of idea further, Amazon also uses customers' browsing and buying records to present lists like 'Customers who bought this item also bought' and 'Customers who viewed this item also viewed'. But customers do not have to do anything to have this information recorded.

Allowing contemporaneous recording by the individual

Contemporaneous recording can be done at the time that things are happening. It may be done with relatively little thought, as there may be little or no reflection time between what happens and recording it. One such possibility is people making audio or video recordings. Normally, such contemporaneous records would need to be processed later at some point, to select, to add context, and to do whatever is needed to make the information into a useful long-term record.

The hardware and software both play a vital part in facilitating this. The hardware must be there when things are happening. If you are already sitting in front of a computer, perhaps studying or interacting with fellow learners, this is not a problem. But if you are out and about, some kind of mobile device is needed – perhaps your mobile phone. The input techniques may still be problematic. Voice input is unlikely to be recognised in noisy environments, and keyboard input is usually very slow. Effective interaction may therefore rely on minimising the amount of input needed. This needs very careful design of the screens, forms or particular context for the entries.

From the scenarios in Chapter 2, Avril and Leo might particularly benefit from technology in the workplace to help them make records on the spot.

Facilitating asynchronous recording and reflection by the holder

Making records after the event is much less of a challenge in hardware terms: any computer that a learner can access at some time may be adequate. However, this requires the portfolio holder to recall things in order to record them. From the holder's perspective, this function is complementary to the contemporaneous recording, although it is categorised separately here because it is not just about the mechanics of recording.

Facilitating feedback and comment from others

From a technical perspective, a very similar function is to allow input from other people. This will, of course, depend on whether others have been allowed to view the original records, and is part of the communicative processes related to the portfolio.

Storing information in general, whether centrally or distributed

In general, portfolio information needs to be stored in a place and a form that can be readily retrieved and reused when needed.

Arguably, for some relevant practice, particularly reflection, there is no need to store information, as the process of reflection is sufficient without any records. But this takes us away from the discussion about e-portfolio systems, so it is not relevant here.

Storage can be localised, centralised or distributed, as mentioned above. It is becoming less important exactly where information is stored, as more storage is constantly networked.

For learners in the workplace, the question of storage can be problematic. In the health-related professions, work-based systems are often made deliberately difficult to access from outside, to help guard against loss of sensitive personal information relating to patients. Thus, for scenarios like that of Leo in Chapter 2, it may not be easy to arrange for an e-portfolio system to be available both on the job and off. For examples like Nadia and the financial services industry, the motivation for guarding information may be partly economic, so as not to allow competitors to see commercially confidential data, and partly personal, to prevent access to clients' financial details. In both cases, some careful design may be needed to balance the need for confidentiality with the desire to allow employees to work on personal and professional development in their own time, as well as in work.

Management, maintenance and elaboration functions

This has rather different connotations for the two kinds of information that can be connected with portfolios: first, the information directly under the learner's control; and second, the unaltered information held by other parties which is provided to the learner for reflection and presentation to others.

Displaying stored information to the holder

Portfolio systems must in all cases allow the holders to view the information that is stored about them. It is easily stated, but also surprisingly easy to fail to do. Information can be obscured by being difficult to access; by being available only in one place, on one machine; by the holder having to remember yet another username and password to access it; and by being inaccessible in terms of the holder's natural ability or special needs.

Allowing editing and deletion of the information stored

The permission to edit and delete clearly depends on what information it is. Some items should not be editable by the individual, if created by an institution or organisation about that individual. This includes exam results and transcripts, and attendance and review records. Material submitted for assessment will normally not be editable, and the assessing body may need to have a reference copy for many purposes, including moderation, disputes, etc. Holders might also have their own copy to work on in parallel.

Adding explicit dates to the records

One particularly useful kind of information concerns dates. Dates of creation, making public, and revision can be stored automatically by an e-portfolio system; however, if the records are about particular occasions, events, activities, experiences, achievements, goals or plans, there may be one or more dates that can be explicitly related to those records. This will allow the records to be ordered and related by the dates to which they refer.

Recording information relationships and making links

Related to the educative purpose of learning about evidence, learners must be allowed to link together claims (e.g. the possession of abilities) with evidence for those claims. Many other kinds of link are possible and relevant, such as linking goals with the activities that contributed to those goals, although this could be seen as part of the function of action planning and goal management.

Linking records may be a particular challenge if the portfolio information is distributed and the two records are on different systems. Nonetheless, it is important so that the records can be reflected on and presented together.

Managing goals and planned actions

Personally, I am very surprised that no systems are readily available at the time of writing that integrate the normal agenda/calendar functionality together with portfolio functionality. It would seem to me ideal to integrate calendars, and indeed address books, with recording and reflection. But, given that the normal calendar functions are performed elsewhere, the role of portfolio systems tends to be to help with what is normally thought of as action planning.

To manage goals and planned actions involves recording goals, recording what sub-goals may contribute to those goals, and what actions or activities go towards fulfilling goals at any level. When a goal has been achieved, the holder needs to be able to mark it as having been achieved, perhaps with some reflective comment on the achievement and how it compares with the original goal.

Information grouping for communication

When a portfolio holder has learned about what particular audiences want to know, there needs to be a method, within portfolio systems, for grouping together sets of portfolio information for those particular audiences. This is true even for CVs, which are classic cases of information communicated as a unit.

With traditional CVs, there is also the task of providing a very short 'headline' for each entry, so that the whole CV can be quickly scanned by other people. For a richer view, it should be possible to link the headline to a fuller entry.

As the awareness and use of distinct personalities develops, portfolio systems may also offer the function of grouping together items on the basis of the relevant personality. This could then make the selection of information for many audiences much easier, as it would simply display an appropriate selection of personality attributes.

Personally-defined tagging

One practice that has become very common, particularly with so-called 'Web 2.0' tools, is to tag things with a word or short phrase. This may include blog entries in a blogging system, photos in a photograph management system (e.g. Flickr, which was one of the first to attract mass usage), or videos in a service such as YouTube. The practice has provoked much comment and debate. It is not equivalent to classification by librarians or information professionals, and has many inherent problems such as language, misspellings, homonyms, synonyms, etc., if used (as it is) across different people's information. But when used just for oneself, it can be a useful way of picking out different categories of personal significance, across a lot of varied material.

The practice of tagging has something in common with information grouping, although grouping with tags is at least initially more for oneself than for others. It also has something in common with recording information relationships. Instead of explicitly recording the relationships between items of portfolio information, a tag associates a set of items, without saying what the connection is. The implication is that all the items share something in common.

An e-portfolio system may also provide pre-arranged labels, like tags, for categorisation according to schemes envisaged by the owners of the system. These 'official' tags may or may not be used by individuals.

Whether the tags are official or personal, they might potentially be used as the basis for grouping information, and for permissions for the groups. For instance, a sophisticated e-portfolio system might (in the future) be able to hold the rule that anything I tag 'private' is not to be shown to other people under any normal circumstances.

Constructing linked narratives

Supporting this function means allowing learners to create narratives which include proper links to detail and evidence, allowing presentational narratives to be written with links that tie together various other information items and artefacts.

Reuse and communication functions

This covers reuse of the information in presentation, feedback and review, and communication with others.

Managing permissions to view, comment, and give feedback

Unless the portfolio is for a single kind of use, and for a uniform audience, the holder will want to display different things for different purposes. This could either be through explicit selection of sets of portfolio items, as above, or it could be through the setting of permissions for items which are intended for communication to or use with other people.

In the very simplest web-based portfolio systems, everything is public, and this is not adequate for many personal development purposes, nor for maintaining distinct identities. Permission systems should allow more detailed distinctions than the simple one between 'public' and 'private', and should allow portfolio holders to grant and retract permission to individuals and to groups for individual portfolio items and for groups of items.

One common distinction is between the kind of people whose role is to help you with portfolio-related activities and learning, and peers, who are in a similar situation to yourself. It may be useful to allow permissions to be set differently for people in these different roles.

When other people have seen one of your portfolios, or some of the material from a portfolio, it is often desirable for them to be able to provide comments or feedback. Although this could be done outside a portfolio system, for instance by word of mouth or e-mail, it is also useful to allow them to use the portfolio system, so that the holder has the information and the feedback readily available together. Most blogging systems allow this. It may also make sense to allow the holder to control whether or not others are allowed to make comments, and whether these comments are in turn available to others, either immediately, or after the holder has approved them.

Review

There may be related processes that go beyond simple feedback from readers. One possibility is for the portfolio system itself to offer automated feedback, based on rules devised by the system's creators. This could be helpful in many situations where another person is not readily available.

Another possibility is that there is a human process that is more structured or formal than simple feedback. However, there is no obvious categorisation of different review processes, and portfolio system builders would have to devise a system for supporting different kinds of review on a case-by-case basis, or provide a tool for administrators to create such processes.

Wider communication and collaboration

Beyond the commenting, feedback and review covered above, an e-portfolio tool might provide more general communication facilities, similar to e-mail and instant messaging. Although these could be provided outside the system, there might be a potential for integrating these services with the portfolio tool, in the same way that social software also integrates these functions. This can provide a highly significant input to personal decision processes, and to the development of personality and social skills.

10

Applying e-portfolio principles

In Part 2, I will set out practical advice for several areas of application. Here, in between covering the principles and moving on to practical advice, I make some general points about bringing together the ideas of purpose, information and functionality, using the example of education.

Education – or perhaps the broader current term, 'learning, education and training' – is an obvious place to start thinking about the application of e-portfolio tools, partly because many such tools have grown up in an educational context. The interplay of purpose, information and functionality could be considered in any area of application, but I will be content with one good example for this book. However, a word of caution would be appropriate. I am not setting out answers about how to apply e-portfolios to education. The answer to that depends heavily on your educational purposes, and within that, what it is practical to implement.

What is the purpose?

Putting purposes in first place fits both with the order of presentation in Part 1 of this book, and with the general principle that purpose is the most important factor, and should be considered first. A review of the possible purposes outlined in earlier chapters is likely to turn up many, if not all, of the purposes that you plan to further with the aid of portfolio tools. Pragmatically, however, you might also start either from a consideration of what information is actually available, or what functionality is proposed.

In education, there are many purposes. One of the most significant factors affecting purposes is whether or not the learning is institutionally designed. The less structure is set out in advance by the learning design, the more general the educational purposes of the institution are likely to be. Conversely, where the structure is laid out in advance, the purposes envisaged by the institution can be as specific and particular as one is able to plan for. The reflective purposes mentioned in Chapter 5 may be ones that feature for planned and unplanned learning. Assessment, both summative and formative, is another purpose within education which is often connected with e-portfolio tools. If your institution takes personal development planning seriously, then supporting personal development planning (PDP) may be on the agenda. Alternatively, you may want to focus on supporting learning processes and objectives. Let's look at some of these in a little more detail.

Helping to reach learning objectives

An educational process could have as its justifiable aim or objective anything that is beneficial for the learner and involves gaining some knowledge or ability. This includes things known generally as educational objectives, and the related, more specific, targeted learning outcomes; other terms may also exist. To integrate best with portfolio tools, learning objectives or outcomes should be defined somewhere that is easily visible to the learners, and that can be accessed by their portfolio tools.

A special case of learning objectives involving e-portfolio tools would be if any of the objectives related to the e-portfolio tools themselves. For instance, an objective might involve the direct use of e-portfolio tools, concern attitudes to portfolio use, or relate to the ability to record experiences, reflect on them, or use the results of reflection in presentations to others. Another objective directly related to e-portfolio practice would be the ability to document and demonstrate personal abilities.

Assessment

Alongside learning objectives, the designers of structured educational processes have to decide on the role of assessment in ensuring the objectives are reached. Final or summative assessment may involve portfolios of work, or a system which helps to administer the collection, presentation and assessment of work. This is a significant area in its own right, and will be dealt with in Chapter 11.

Formative assessment could be seen as another kind of learning process.

Supporting learning processes

In principle, it is possible to allow learners to choose how to meet learning objectives. However, many courses design the process to a greater or lesser extent, or at least envisage how the learning process might take place. If the processes are designed, they may involve materials and tools. Some of these tools may be portfolio tools. Processes, and thus tools, will depend greatly on the kinds of learning objectives selected.

Learners also might wish to plan the learning processes they undertake, and thus the tools that they use. There is clearly plenty of scope for supporting this choice. Alternatively, there may be reasons for requiring learners to use a particular e-portfolio system for unstructured learning, simply to make it easier for staff to access the materials and records they assemble.

Supporting personal development

Educational institutions often take seriously the task of supporting the personal development of their learners. This may be just because it is a good thing to do, and may generate positive publicity, or it may be because it is a requirement dictated by government policy (as, to an extent, for UK higher education). E-portfolio tools have a long track record here, so it is not difficult to connect this purpose to the portfolio world. Alternatively, personal development may be conceived of as developing the set of skills needed to be an effective, independent learner, with the ability to succeed as a learner in that institution.

Supporting employability

Supporting employability is also common in educational institutions. It is not wholly separate from supporting personal development, but rather something similar from a different point of view, in cases where the learner is concerned about employability.

What information is relevant?

When we talk about information in the context of education, we need to remember the point made in Chapter 6, that information, for an e-portfolio system, means anything that can be recorded and stored in that system, including anything that a learner might put into words, such as thoughts, feelings, opinions or reflections, in addition to any work that a learner might do as part of an educational course.

On the whole, when the purposes are clear, it will be possible to clarify the information relevant to those purposes. A general way of doing this might be to find or decide some methods of achieving the purposes, break down those methods into steps, focus on the decisions or actions taken at each step, and work out what information is relevant to informing each decision or action. One can then think about where that information is. Some information may be generated or stored electronically; some may be on paper; some may exist only in people's heads.

We can think of educational examples in terms of the purposes above. To help learners reach learning objectives, a portfolio system could record the results of any assessments relevant to the learning objectives, particularly formative assessments, so that the learner can check their progress at any time. This record could be as simple as a checklist of outcomes achieved. In a portfolio setting, it is likely that an educational institution would seek to complement its own testing by also offering self-assessment. This might be in the form of self-testing, where records of the results of self-administered tests are kept in the portfolio system, so that they can be made available to advisers, to help the learner make decisions about learning.

Summative assessment is in some ways easier, because fairness in summative assessment requires being clear about how the assessment is carried out, and what counts. In summative assessment of vocational education or training, the main piece of information may just be ticks or checks from a relevant assessor, to say that each particular outcome has been demonstrated.

The information involved with supporting personal development may, in contrast, be less clear, as it very much depends on the scope of the current conception of personal development in the institution.

Supporting employability has at least two areas of relevant information: employability skills, which are often covered in PDP, and the actual information that a learner will want to assemble for application forms, for CVs, and for e-portfolios presenting skills to potential employers. In addition to information assembled by the learner, the results of assessments and any other reports carried out or created by the institution may also be relevant.

Instead of working initially from purposes, another approach is to consider what information is available at present, and then to make a judgment about whether there might be a portfolio-related purpose in using it. In Chapter 6, we looked in depth at the kinds of information that might reasonably play a part in e-portfolio systems. But it is perhaps more straightforward to look at the information that is stored in existing information systems.

Information stored in dedicated e-portfolio systems is not difficult to consider, but other information may not be so obvious. Educational institutions all have some kind of files on their pupils or students, and these may contain much that is of potential relevance to the kinds of purposes that we have considered. Names, addresses, other contact details, etc., can in principle be passed on to portfolio systems to use in presentation to others. Reports and the results of examinations, tests and assessments are often stored somewhere, and all of these are potentially valuable for reflection, and for presentation to others as evidence.

The fact that information is held in some information system is no guarantee that it can be extracted or reused. Indeed, the interoperability of student record systems and portfolio systems is ripe for development. But at least recognising the information that is there will be important, even if only to note what procedures need to be put in place to allow the information to be passed on as appropriate, and to try to ensure that information from one source does not conflict with information from another.

What functionality is helpful?

There are three reasonable starting points for considering functionality, none of which can be relied upon alone to give clear answers.

One can, again, start from the purposes, and consider what the user of an information system must be able to do to further those purposes. For example, for assessment, a learner needs to check what has been assessed already, and what is on the agenda for assessment. When the time comes, the learner needs to be able to upload evidence into an area where it can be assessed. Assessors need to be able to see material that has been presented for assessment, record marks, and perhaps note feedback for the learner.

For personal development, or for employability, the learner will probably be set exercises to carry out. Some of these may involve looking back at things written previously, writing about what has been done and achieved in the past. If e-portfolio systems are more generally to be used to help towards educational objectives, then the learner needs to be able to see those objectives, and their progress towards them. Actions which contribute towards the objectives may need to be entered or recorded in some way.

Another way is to start from the information. As per the previous chapter, one can see the portfolio functions as essentially the capture, management and output of portfolio information. As such, the functionality may be seen in terms of that distinction. The actual functionality which emerges from this process may not be any different from the functionality that emerges from a consideration of purpose, but if the same things do come up, at least there will be the added assurance that the same functionality looks right from two separate perspectives.

A third approach is to base future functionality on what has happened in the past. This includes the very common situation that certain processes were once carried out on paper, but there is now a reason for wanting to do them electronically. Two starting points for this are what is available in e-learning tools, and what has been done as PDP using paper. Of course, this approach by itself will not give any new ideas, but it is probably good to check whether what was held as useful in the past should continue to be supported in the future.

There is thus no clear answer to the question of what should be addressed first: purpose, information or functionality. If you decide to prioritise the consideration of information, this may limit the functionality that you can offer through the electronic tools. Equally, you may decide that the case for certain functionality is so strong that you will try harder to make the necessary information available electronically.

On the other hand, if you want to give priority to functionality, you may find that the information required to support that functionality is not practically available electronically, and your ideas of functionality will need to be revised.

Tools for education

A rational approach to decide on what portfolio tools to use in an educational context might proceed by evaluating the available tools, based on the joint approach described above, covering purpose, information and functionality.

It is safest to disregard the fact of whether the term 'e-portfolio' is used in the tool description. Much more reliable is to go through a process, starting with the consideration of which functions need to be supported, continuing with selecting the functions that are to be supported by information and communications systems, and finishing by evaluating possible tools on the basis of which parts of the required functionality they cover, and how easy they are for the intended learners to use. We may think of tools that support at least some of the functionality we want as 'portfolio-related' tools, whether or not those who built the systems use the term 'e-portfolio'.

There are several options for how portfolio-related tools may be implemented. Software may be installed on specific computers, or given to learners to install on their own machines. Alternatively, a portfolio service may be installed on a server which is accessible through the hardware used by the learners. Most commonly at present, the software can be made available as a website that learners can access from anywhere with an internet connection, given their own username and password. Moreover, a portfolio tool may be a single system with a single database, or it may have different parts which may be accessed separately, or through one single 'front end' or 'portal'.

For learning that is not structured or planned, the role of e-portfolio tools is harder to define. Because the actual use of the personal information may not have been decided in advance, one is left with the option of collecting such information as may be potentially useful for the envisaged generic uses. The choice of what information to collect in the learners' portfolios will probably need to be backed up by a significant amount of education and motivation of the learners, and that may well itself be structured. A reasonable strategy for choosing tools in this situation may be to try out different approaches and reflect on the experiences.

Summary

This has been a very short illustration of the principles of Part 1, as applied to education. I haven't made it longer because it would be very easy to be drawn into particular issues that more concern education than e-portfolios. The references given below include up-to-date (at the time of writing) discussions and illustrations of e-portfolio concepts applied to education, particularly higher education.

References and further reading

Aalderink, W. and Veugelers, M. (eds) (2007) 'Stimulating lifelong learning: the e-portfolio in Dutch higher education', available at: *http://www.surffoundation.nl/smartsite.dws?ch=eng&id=13319*.

Cambridge, B. (ed.) (2001) *Electronic Portfolios: Emerging Practices in Student, Faculty and Institutional Learning*.

Cambridge, D., Cambridge, B. and Yancey, K. B. (2008) *Electronic Portfolios 2.0: Emergent Research on Implementation and Impact.*

Hallam, G. (project leader) et al. (2008) 'Australian ePortfolio Project – final project report', available at: *http://www.eportfoliopractice.qut.edu.au/information/report/index.jsp.*

JISC (2008) 'Effective practice with e-portfolios', available at: *http://www.jisc.ac.uk/whatwedo/themes/elearning/eportfolios/effectivepracticeeportfolios.aspx.*

JISC infoNet (2008) 'e-Portfolios infoKit', available at: *http://www.jiscinfonet.ac.uk/e-portfolios.*

Part 2:
How to do things with e-portfolio and related tools

Introduction to this part

While the chapters of Part 1 deal with the principles, and relate to the three themes of purpose, information and functionality, when it comes to addressing 'how to' questions, none of those three themes by themselves provide adequate answers. In this part of the book, my intention is to be both helpful and relatively brief, cutting across whatever themes and issues are necessary to give you what presently seems to be good advice. However, 'how to' guides cannot always give a simple formula for how to do everything, and often need to be content with pointing out issues and suggesting ways to resolve them. The chapters in this section tend towards this method.

Each chapter is structured along similar lines. First, there is a general review of the chapter heading subject. Some of the topics are familiar and need no introduction, while others merit a few paragraphs, as the principles may not be known, and may not have been dealt with properly in Part 1.

The following section is called 'Perspectives'. I want to make it clear whose point of view is being represented in each chapter. The different readers of this book will have different interests, and the chapters are all primarily aimed at certain specific groups. When I write 'you' in one of these chapters, you can check who 'you' might be by referring back to this section of the chapter. I also connect back to the scenarios in Chapter 2, which all give possible individual perspectives.

After we have clarified for whom the chapter has been written, I describe why you might be interested in the chapter topic. I hope I have covered many of the important reasons for being interested. If you feel I have overlooked your interests then I would be interested to know.

Next comes the first of the two most substantial sections: 'Questions to think about'. These are the questions that I feel are the most important when thinking about the chapter topic, and the answers are designed to inform any decisions you take. Particularly in a new area, it is easy to miss some important questions, and I hope my listing makes the issues harder to miss and the real task easier.

After you have considered the questions, you will be in a better position to make decisions about the actions you want to take. I divide relevant points into two sections, if appropriate. 'Choice of tools' reviews some considerations which might be useful if the chapter topic naturally leads on to choosing an e-portfolio tool. 'Other action points to consider' covers other useful or important actions you way wish to pursue.

'Summary of relevant principles' is where I may refer back, particularly if I haven't already done so in the body of the text, to the chapters in Part 1 which are relevant to the chapter here in Part 2. Sometimes there is one particularly relevant chapter, sometimes a few. Occasionally, all of Part 1 is relevant to a chapter here.

Finally, there may be chapter references giving details of works I cite in the text, and any notes. If I know of any, I include also related material that is worth reading for other or deeper treatment of the same topics, even if I don't cite them. Academics will perhaps notice that I choose not to use the full academic referencing customs. This is because I expect readers who want to find references to be looking initially on the web. I try always to give enough information so that a web search will bring up the reference at or near the top, or if not, I give a URL or other fuller reference. I don't mention Wikipedia in the references, not because it isn't useful – it is very useful – but because I assume you will look up things on Wikipedia (or any other similar useful source of web-based information) in any case.

How to choose an e-portfolio system

I should make it plain at this point that I am not going to answer this question directly, because I maintain that there is no simple answer to the question in general. If you have read Part 1, you will not be surprised to know that the answer to that question depends on the purposes you or your users have in mind, the information that is available to your users, and the functionality that is required, needed or wanted. However, the choice is not dependent on any one of these alone. It is better tackled through the following 'how-to' questions, where in many cases the question of choice of system for a particular situation is addressed.

There is, however, one question that cuts across most of the chapters in this part, and this follows here.

Commercial or free/open source?

If, after you have taken all the considerations in any relevant chapters into account, you decide you want to have an e-portfolio system, there is one major choice that cuts across many other issues: whether to choose a system based on commercial or on open source software. Both have advantages and drawbacks.

Commercial software relieves you of any need to worry about the workings of the system. Your relationship with the vendor is transactional and contractual: you pay them money, they deliver you the service you pay for. If it doesn't work satisfactorily, you have someone to complain to: no one in your organisation or institution needs to understand the details of how their software works. In addition, when the system is improved, you may get the improvements without asking. On the negative side, there is no guarantee that the improvements you want are high on your supplier's list of priorities. Then, what do you do if they stop providing the service, withdraw support, or even disappear as a business? What happens if they unexpectedly decide to raise their charges – would you be 'locked in'? And can people in your organisation freely use the information that is stored in the e-portfolio system for other purposes? If you didn't ensure this in the contract, the information stored may be very difficult to extract, and in any case it may be little use if it is not in an interoperable format. The financial 'bottom line' is that commercial software costs money for licences, but relieves you of the expenses for looking after the system.

Free, or open source software needs your organisation to take more responsibility, as there is no vendor to get back to. You will need access to the resources to build and install the software, fix any problems, and make any adaptations or improvements. On the other hand, this is allowed. If you choose a popular tool, there will be other organisations in potentially similar situations, and you may be able to share the costs and effort of maintenance and development. Your institution will have control of any information entered, and you can pass on appropriate control to the learners. Open source software is free of charges and restrictions: the costs will usually be in the staff time required to do what is necessary to look after the software and the installation.

There are middle ways: some commercial organisations will offer to manage free or open source software for you, for payment. You could compare the cost of such a contract with the cost of a commercial software licence, and compare these 'total costs of ownership' with the total cost of providing resources in-house.

11

How to use tools for assessment

Assessment is a process that happens in different ways for different purposes, but all share the common thread that someone rates or gives feedback on someone's ability or abilities in selected areas, on the basis of selected evidence. I take it first here because assessment in one form or another always has been, and still is, central to e-portfolio purposes. Here are some of the different approaches to assessment:

- official assessors can mark or grade people, producing criteria for any relevant selection process;
- teachers or educators can give feedback aimed at improving learners' achievements;
- learners can assess themselves, for whatever reasons they might have;
- other learners from a peer group can give feedback to a peer;
- colleagues and managers can assess performance at work.

At one end of the spectrum, assessment may be a very well defined process. 'High-stakes' assessment – that is, assessment where much of importance hangs on its outcome – tends to be well-defined, in an effort towards fairness, because fairness is difficult to assure without clear definitions. Traditional examinations may have many failings, but at least they are relatively well defined, often in terms of the ability of the candidate to answer questions 'on the spot'. Where many people are going through the same assessment process, fairness is also helped if the questions are ones that everyone has an equal chance of being able to answer. If questions rely on the detail of individual experience, or a particular cultural background, it is more difficult to ensure this fairness.

As well as knowledge, the ability to perform some tasks can also be assessed in a well-defined way, through standardised procedures, as in the medical Objective Structured Clinical Examination. This approach tends to be used for skills that are themselves well-defined, and where it is clear what counts as evidence of the ability in practice. It does not need any records of past experience to be stored or brought up for assessment.

There are other skills which it is less easy to assess in a well-defined way. Take, for example, the ability to work with others in teams. This is not something that can be assessed reliably on the basis of answering questions about what should be done in different situations, as you may know in theory what to do but be unable to carry it out in practice. Nor is it likely to be a fair assessment to put you in a role-playing situation for a few minutes to see how you cope. Team-working ability tends to come out in situations where there is a real goal, and where you have been able to get to know the other team members. Thus, to assess the ability, it makes sense to refer back to experiences where you were actually working in a team, and to assess how you got on then. Several different kinds of evidence may be relevant. For instance, you could ask for feedback from others in your team, or you could assess the outcome of the task in which your team was engaged. Your tutor, or the system, could ask you to describe critical incidents and how you handled them, and these could be checked against reports from other members of your team.

Another approach to this would be through what are known as assessment centres or selection centres. Some employers rely on the results of candidates attending assessment centres to help them select appropriate employees. But while practical exercises would certainly seem better than written or spoken tests, it is much more difficult to know the extent to which a one or two-day exercise reflects real potential in longer-term relationships in the workplace.

The assessment of artistic talent is another example where portfolios have been used traditionally. This clearly has little to do with the ability to answer questions on the spot, which would be more relevant to the art critic than the artist. In addition, abilities which are demonstrable within the timescale of an examination (perhaps like portrait sketching) cover only a part of artistic talent. Here, the accepted approach to assessment is to present works of art, possibly together with explanations giving their context, background or meaning for the artist.

The obvious approach to assessment in situations such as these, where there are no obviously well-defined examination processes, is to gather together evidence, present it to assessors, and for the assessors to assess the evidence presented. This is the essence of a portfolio approach to assessment, and applies as much to self-assessment as it does to assessment by others.

Perspectives

To many people, the most obvious perspective on assessment will be that of the educational institution. Institutions are traditionally associated first with teaching knowledge, and sometimes training skill; second, with assessing the learning that has taken place, summatively; and third, with defending the reputation of the qualifications that are offered as a result of the assessments. As they want their learners to succeed, institutions also have an interest in formative assessment while courses are in progress. In many ways, traditionally including tests and tutorials, institutions assess where learners have reached, and can then vary the educational experience in an attempt to ensure that the learner is able to complete their summative assessments satisfactorily. Professional bodies may have a similar perspective.

It would make sense for learners themselves to be interested in formative assessment, whether managed by the institution or by themselves. The main difference is that whereas institutions are liable to focus on the officially-recognised learning that is part of their formal offering, learners themselves may have a wider range of objectives and levels. The results of personal formative assessment do not necessarily coincide with the results of institutional formative assessment. Perhaps this is why some learners seem uninterested in the formative assessment on offer.

Of the scenarios in Chapter 2, all but the last one (Nadia) are involved in some kind of assessment, from the perspective of the individuals being assessed.

Why do you want to do this?

You have a suitable assessment requirement

You may have a requirement for assessment that cannot easily be fulfilled by traditional tests. There may be evidence that can conveniently be gathered together with an e-portfolio system to be presented for assessment. Alternatively, it may be that you wish to investigate the potential and suitability of an e-portfolio component for your assessment.

You already have an e-portfolio assessment strategy

One step further down the line, you may have already decided that e-portfolio assessment is the way to go for your assessment needs, but how to do this is not clear. Alternatively, the decision to adopt an e-portfolio approach may have been taken by someone above you.

You have an e-portfolio system

Perhaps there is already an e-portfolio system in use in your institution or organisation, but you don't know how to use it for assessment. You want to consider how it might be used for assessment.

You want to assess yourself

You want to assess your own ability in some area where simpler tests are not applicable, or not appropriate, and you are considering a portfolio approach.

Questions to think about

What are the purposes and outcomes of the assessment?

It makes sense to start with the purpose of the assessment. Assessment purposes are often grouped into 'formative', or assessment *for* learning, and 'summative', or assessment *of* learning. You may be able to say much more about your purposes. Purposes are linked to outcomes: for example, if the purpose is to act as a measure for use in selection, one outcome of the assessment process will be that some people are accepted and others rejected. This leads on to considering what the stakes are; for example, hiring an unsuitable employee may cost a lot of money, while allowing unsuitable people onto a course may lower the attainment of the learners as a whole, or increase the drop-out rate. Knowing what is at stake will help decisions about how much resource can or should be devoted to assessment, and resources may potentially be a limiting factor for portfolio-based assessment.

There are a host of other pedagogical purposes which could be furthered by using e-portfolios for assessment.

Do you want assessment only, or assessment with development?

Once you have clarified your overall purposes, you can ask yourself whether you want a tool that only tests and grades learners, or whether you also want to use the broader developmental potential of e-portfolio tools. There are what have been called 'assessment management systems', which are commonly used in the (summative) assessment of National Vocational Qualifications (NVQs). (This is the Avril scenario in Chapter 2.) If you want people to use their assessment processes or results for their personal or professional development, you might want a system that includes some of the functionality common to the many e-portfolio tools used for this, but you will have to check whether the assessment and development functions work together effectively.

What characteristics of people do you wish to assess?

You may want to start with this question, as an alternative. Traditional paper-based examinations have tended to emphasise the assessment of someone's knowledge, or more exactly, their ability to recall or use certain knowledge explicitly on demand, typically in a context quite different from where the knowledge would be used in practice. Where skills are involved, traditional examinations focus on the knowledge that underlies the skill, or the use of the skill. Practical tests focus on abilities themselves (skills, competence, etc.), and the capacity to display that ability in the assessment context. Do you want to assess this kind of thing, or is it something where evidence needs to be gathered?

Is context important to assessment?

Is the characteristic you wish to assess something that is dependent on context, or where the situation in which it is displayed develops over time? If so, then a portfolio approach may be worth investigating. If it is something that is reliably displayed, for instance, by multiple choice tests, then there is little point in using the more time-consuming portfolio approach.

How could those candidates' characteristics be assessed?

Rationally, you can start by reviewing the possible ways of assessing candidates' characteristics, then choose those most appropriate to the situation, given some criteria of appropriateness. Many writers have set out ranges of assessment methods, or approaches to assessment, so it is easy to check whether an obvious option, or alternative to portfolio assessment, has been missed.

What information is to be used in the assessment process?

From the point of view of an e-portfolio system, it is important to be clear about exactly what will play a part in the assessment, so that you can check that the portfolio systems can hold that information. Is it blog entries, essays or coursework; other artefacts such as photographs or video or audio files; various things linked together through a web page (or equivalent); records of interactions, conversations, etc.; or comments by others? The different kinds of evidence may need different kinds of technical provision.

Who is going to be involved in the assessment process?

The complete assessment process in your organisation or institution needs to fit with the capabilities of the e-portfolio system. For instance, one issue that could easily be overlooked is the matter of who is involved in the process as a whole. Is it just learners and teachers/assessors, or are there other roles? If not designed with care, there can be a mismatch between information systems on the one hand and established organisational processes and workflows on the other.

What are the motives that suggest an electronic (rather than paper) approach?

There may be a temptation to adopt e-portfolio tools because they are seen as smart, modern, cool, green, etc. But there are real possible benefits, particularly for formal assessment processes. For example, some research in 2007 by FreshMinds for ACER, the Association of Colleges in the Eastern Region (of England) found that: 'Increased efficiency, better use of assessor time, and speeding up achievement process were among the most frequently cited benefits of e-portfolio systems'. Their report details many benefits and problems in the area covered, namely the summative approach to NVQ assessment.

If you already use a paper portfolio approach to assessment, you will need to carefully weigh up the costs and benefits of moving from paper to electronic. If you have a need for a portfolio approach, but have no portfolio processes in place, the balance is more in favour of an e-portfolio approach, as there is no paper alternative with which to stay.

Choice of tools

Assess whether existing tools offer the functionality required for assessment

There have been many surveys and reports in recent years covering e-portfolio tools, so it should not be difficult to obtain a current list of products (commercial and open source) through a combination of looking at surveys, searching and asking around. You should, however, be aware that people whose interests are in personal development may not know about assessment management e-portfolio systems, and those interested just in vocational assessment may not know about the developmental potential of e-portfolios. In the light of the considerations above, you should have a good start on evaluating different tools, or combinations of tools if no one tool alone is adequate. You can look at both the actions that are allowed in the system, and the information that can be stored.

Building your own assessment-related portfolio tool

If there is any software available that is close to your requirements, or even adaptable to them, the advice you will get from most experienced people is not to try putting together your own bespoke system. Creating your own system means not only committing to the effort of writing any necessary code, but also of testing, maintaining and improving the system as a whole.

If you insist on building your own e-portfolio system, you may need to take into account the following points at the very least:

- The system will need storage space where learners assemble material for assessment, private to the learner. You will need to work out how much space you need, based on any files that the learners may be allowed to store.

- The system will need a way of displaying the abilities (etc.) that are to be demonstrated in the assessment framework.

- Learners will need to be able to link the files they upload, reflections, and any other writings, to the assessment framework.
- If you are doing summative assessment, there has to be a way of 'freezing' the portfolio when submitted, or at a deadline. One way of doing this would be to take a complete copy into an area where the learners cannot edit it.
- Assessors need to have access to all relevant information and files, and to be able to leave marks and comments, some of which should be for feedback to the learner.
- If moderators are involved, they will need read-access to the all the information stored.
- Security will need to be in place to ensure that unauthorised people do not get access. The strength of the security should be proportionate to the stakes of the assessment.
- If the information to be assessed includes any comments, feedback or contributions by others, the system may need to allow others to give their permission, and to record that permission.
- The system may need to provide for communication between learners and assessors about the assessment process, and about feedback and results.

Other action points to consider

Security

Security has been mentioned above as a consideration if you build your own system, but it needs a thorough treatment in any case, proportionate to the stakes in the assessment. Security cannot simply be delegated to system vendors, as a large part of security rests on procedures within the organisation or institution, and cannot be fully covered simply by technical means.

Accessibility

Whether assessment is going to be offered as a service, or is an integral part of a course, the processes must be accessible to all relevant learners. Some of this should be covered by a vendor, but it will be the responsibility of the institution or organisation to ensure it is properly covered.

Summary of relevant principles

Refer to Chapter 5 for deeper discussion of purposes in general. It is essential to clarify what you are trying to achieve through assessment with e-portfolios.

The information that can be seen as relevant to e-portfolio systems is covered in detail in Chapter 6. This should help in reviewing and deciding what information might be used as part of an e-portfolio assessment process.

The issues in Chapter 7 are all relevant here. Data protection is essential, as all assessment information is personal to individuals. Authentication and verification have an important role to play for high-stakes assessment and the presentation of results to others. Interoperability will be important if more than one system is involved, or if there is any desire to reuse the information collected for assessment in other contexts, which is quite possible. Interoperability can be built in for systems that are created or modified in-house, or it can be required from vendors. The notes on centralised or distributed storage may help with system design.

The discussion of common terms in Chapter 8 becomes important, particularly if the assessment is meant to relate to the interests of other parties – for example, if employability or vocational skills are being assessed in an academic context.

References and further reading

There are various discussions available about assessment with portfolios. Searching the web with the terms 'portfolio' and 'assessment' together yields many links. Likewise, a web search for 'assessment methods' will bring up many websites relevant to assessment in general.

The report cited in this chapter is FreshMinds (2007) 'NVQ portfolio assessment methods: Alternatives to current practices'. Although this is not presently available on the web, there are other useful resources. These include a directory of assessment portfolio system suppliers (*http://www.nvqweb.com/resource_directory/eassessment*) and a list of resources maintained by Helen Barrett, the self-styled 'grandmother' of the e-portfolio world (*http://electronicportfolios.com/portfolios.html*).

The Learning and Teaching Support Network Generic Centre has published a guide by David Baume (2003) 'Supporting portfolio development', available at: *http://www.heacademy.ac.uk/assets/York/documents/resources/resourcedatabase/id295_Supporting_Portfolio_Development.pdf*.

The REAP project 'Re-Engineering Assessment Practices in Scottish Higher Education', which finished in 2007, is highly relevant to e-portfolio assessment (*http://www.reap.ac.uk/*)

Finally, I am currently working on a project on the role of e-portfolios in assessment, which will also have a website (*http://www.recordingachievement.org/e-portfolio-assessment/*).

12

How to use tools for recording significant personal information

Information that needs to be recorded for assessment is often well defined, but in many other e-portfolio applications, the question of what to record is more open, though the information that is recorded is still of personal significance. This chapter aims to address all these other uses of portfolios.

I've put the word 'significant' in the chapter title because it flags some important issues. There are many kinds of technology that could be used for recording information connected with an individual. For example, you could make indiscriminate audio or video recordings of your whole life, but this is unlikely to be very helpful. For sensible e-portfolio work, we want to record things connected with ourselves (or others) that have some kind of meaning or significance. It is important to recognise that what is significant is not always entirely obvious. People, particularly young people, may benefit from education about what is significant for others (or indeed for themselves). Furthermore, the extent of that significance will vary from person to person, and from situation to situation.

Perspectives

There are two quite clear and distinct perspectives on recording personal information. One is from the perspective of the person who the information concerns – perhaps you. From this 'self' perspective, as we could call it, it is generally useful to record information for one of two reasons. First, you could record such information to reflect on, in which case anything that you consider significant could be recorded. Second, you might record this information for presentation to or sharing with others, in which case you may have a clear view about what is significant for you and for them; sharing such information with your intended audience will enhance your reputation with them.

The other perspective is for anyone who is not the person related to the information, and in particular, institutional and commercial interests. First and foremost, other people and organisations probably want to keep relevant contact details for you, and details of how to find further information about you in their information systems. These non-portfolio information systems would typically also contain information specifically relevant to the services the organisation has provided for you, and records of the dealings it has had with you – the business relationship history, if you like.

There is plenty of room for conflict between these perspectives. Everyone wants accurate information for their own purposes, in their own terms, but for various reasons you may not want to share accurate information about yourself, or you may not want certain facts about yourself to be stored by other organisations. If there is a sufficiently strong motive, individuals sometimes resort to storing deliberately inaccurate information about themselves, in order to mislead.

The scenarios in Chapter 2 are all from the perspective of the person themself. The information collected by Avril may not seem so significant, as it is primarily directed at summative assessment, but the information collected by all the others is probably of wider significance to them.

Why do you want to do this?

You have a specific use in mind for the information

Perhaps you have a particular reason to store and reuse information, either about yourself or what you have done, or about another person. This is the only acceptable reason for an organisation to keep information about an individual, but when keeping information about yourself, you may or may not have a particular reason. If you have a specific use in mind, most likely there will be some specific information that is relevant to that use, and perhaps other information about which you are not so sure of the relevance.

Quite possibly, the recognition of how information will be used in a specific way may suggest an obvious way of gathering it, so that a general-purpose portfolio is not needed. Information about your expenditure would be simple to collect on a spreadsheet, where it can be added up automatically. Information about medical symptoms might perfectly adequately be kept on notepaper, to be taken to the doctor's. The kind of specific purpose that invites a portfolio approach might be gathering together specific information for presentation to others, using the capabilities of the portfolio tool.

You want to become a more reflective person

Perhaps you have come across the idea that being a reflective person has certain benefits, and you like the idea of those benefits, or you just like the connotations of being more reflective, irrespective of evidence of any particular benefit. As such, you want to collect information focused on your thoughts and experiences, for reflection.

You want to understand yourself and your personality

Many people, at some stages in their lives, have a sense that they don't know who they really are. You may not be aware of what is fundamental to you, as opposed to what is just an aspect or a mask you put on to fit in with particular kinds of situation. You thus want to collect information to help understand yourself, in terms that can help you make sense of yourself. Current tools may offer limited help with this, but much remains to be developed. This topic is discussed further in Part 3.

You like collecting information about yourself

Perhaps you have no explicit purpose, but just feel that you enjoy collecting information about yourself. Perhaps you have the general feeling that it might be of some use one day, or perhaps you like to review it from time to time, without conceiving of this as reflection. Perhaps you have enjoyed writing a diary in the past, and want to write something that is richer, and can hold more, than a plain paper-based diary.

Perhaps another version of this motive applies to the situation where you have to use an e-portfolio system designated by your institution, organisation, or company, and you want to explore what you can record about yourself, without a clear idea of how you want to use it again.

Questions to think about

Are you allowed to keep information about someone else?

No one restricts people from keeping information about themselves, although in some societies it can be risky if the wrong people find out. However, if your organisation wants to record and keep information about other people, you will need to clarify whether this is allowed under data protection legislation. In the UK, at least, it would appear that the legislation is not designed to restrict personal collection of information about other people for purely personal use (see Chapter 7).

What kinds of information are well adapted for electronic storage?

Information that can be represented as text poses no problem for electronic storage. Photographs, encoded digitally, are also simple to store, although they use more storage space. Audio recordings are as straightforward as digital photographs, although there are more varieties of format. Video tends to take much more space, but no other particular issues of principle are raised.

Representations of physical objects, such as photographs, sketches, plans or descriptions can be stored electronically. These representations may act as evidence of the physical reality, although descriptions can be misleading, and photographs can be faked.

What information do you want to store?

This will presumably be your own selection of what it is possible to store, given the purposes you have. If you have no particular purpose, or no particular information in mind, it may just come down to the spur of the moment, and perhaps trial and error, in the sense that if you record something, and later notice or decide it is of no interest or use, you may learn not to bother recording the same kind of information again.

When, where and how do you want to record it?

This affects your choice of technology. For instance, if the largest device you can have with you is a mobile phone, you must ensure that it will do the job you want it to do. If the information then needs to be transferred from a recording device to a storage system, the ease of this transfer needs to be considered. If your desk is a good place for recording the things you want to record, and you are at your desk at appropriate times, then any system available on the internet may work.

Would a simpler storage system be adequate?

This book is not promoting technology for technology's sake. For many purposes, non-electronic or non-portfolio storage may be just as good, if not better. How about a paper diary, notebook, mobile phone or other personal device?

Choice of tools

Choosing a personal approach

For simply recording the information, the above questions will help you think about what approach to take. It is becoming much more common to have several choices of how to record things. As well as traditional paper formats, there is your own personal computer storage, in several formats; your mobile phone (text, images, audio or video on flash memory); or services on the web, including social networking systems and blogs, as well as dedicated e-portfolio systems. Organisations you belong to may provide one or more systems that you could use, or may provide nothing. As such, there is little to be said in general about your choice, except that there are probably more options than would occur to you immediately, so it may be worth considering just how the information is to be used, ensuring you have considered all feasible options, and choosing appropriately.

If, on consideration, none of the tools provided fit what you want to do, one way of using the analysis in this chapter is to suggest appropriate improvements to the people who run an e-portfolio system. The fact that such systems are still very much under development may give an opportunity for the input of personal requirements.

Choosing a system for others in your organisation

If you are in the position of choosing a system for others to use, the above considerations should help your choice. You could, most simply, try to imagine what the perspectives of your users are, or better, you can ask them directly.

Other action points to consider

Using your system

If you have been given an e-portfolio or similar system that you can use, or you can access one of your own choosing, you could find out more about the kinds information you can store in it, and also see whether other people use it for more than what is instructed. Such research may give you more ideas about what you want to store and how you might use it and is worth considering before going through your selection process.

Summary of relevant principles

The most relevant chapter in Part 1 is Chapter 4, which discusses the basic underlying motivation for storing information. Data protection considerations are raised in Chapter 7.

References and further reading

To find more about why someone should think that reflection is beneficial, try searching for 'benefits of reflection' or 'benefits of reflective practice'. As mentioned above in Chapter 5, key authors here include Chris Argyris, Donald Schön and Christopher Johns.

13

How to use tools for self-presentation

Having collected information about yourself, something that calls itself an e-portfolio tool is likely to enable you to select appropriate materials for one or more audiences and purposes, to compose them into a coherent presentation, to ensure that the intended audience can see the presentation, and perhaps to take steps to keep it private from others. What is much less likely is that such a tool could educate you in how best to do this, and this knowledge may need to be sought by interacting with people.

Before the internet was widely used, there was no easy and cheap method of presenting yourself to a wide general audience. Few people had the time or ability to write an autobiography, and getting an autobiography published was not easy, as it would likely not be profitable for publishers. Some technologically-inclined people have used web pages to present themselves to others ever since the web first became available.

Perspectives

The perspective of this chapter is of the individual – you want to present yourself. Helping others to use tools is covered separately, in Chapter 15.

Back in Chapter 2, Bart's self-presentation is aimed at moving on to university. His perspective is less central to the topic here, because the only information he has to think about carefully is his structured personal statement; other headings and structure are provided by an application form. Nadia's perspective is much more central, as she is putting together a range of information for presenting herself to future employers.

Why do you want to do this?

You want a job

You may want just any job, in which case your e-portfolio could contain almost anything about yourself that might make you seem more employable. More likely, you want a particular kind of job, or a job with a particular company or organisation, and so you want to display the kind of information that makes you look attractive to that kind of employer, presenting yourself as a desirable employee, able to perform the job or undertake the role successfully.

You want business

This is very similar to wanting a job: you want to present yourself as a professional or trade person who can and does give clients a service that they want.

You want to attract other individuals for some mutually rewarding interaction

This covers a wide range of reasons, from finding someone to share your life with to finding someone to share a hobby such as music or sport. In each case, you will probably have some idea (even if it is inaccurate) of what the other people might want to know.

You want to display a picture of yourself to the world

You haven't got a particular purpose in mind, and you don't (yet?) want to write a traditional autobiography, but you do want to see what can be done with e-portfolio tools to present a coherent impression of yourself to a general audience. There may be several personal motives behind this, and they might be hard to clarify, but they are probably in line with the motives of people who write extensive personal web pages.

Questions to think about

Who are your audience?

Common possibilities include:

- the public – that is, anyone who has or may take an interest in you for any reason;
- particular people you want to impress;
- others in your workplace, often managers;
- people in one or more of the various social settings you frequent;
- friends and family.

How are you going to reach your audience?

Do the people you want to reach already belong to some company or organisation with its own communication channels, or an established business or social network? Or do you already have a channel of communication open with them, personally? If so it may be worth exploring how to use those established channels.

Will it suffice to simply create some presentation and then send it to your audience, or notify them of where it is? Or would it be more effective to participate in some kind of existing social network, and bring yourself and your information to the attention of the others in that network through the social networking processes, rather than directly?

If you don't know who your audience is, or if you do not share any established communication channels, how are you going to get their attention?

What information about you is relevant to which other people?

If you have only particular people in mind, you can probably just decide on one presentation. But if you are trying to reach various different kinds of people, will you be able to do it through one channel, or do you need a different channel for each different selection of information, or is there a way to have different people using the same channel but seeing different things?

This problem will be particularly difficult if you do not know your audience and you have to be public about the information you present. You will need to present enough information to appeal to your intended audience without presenting anything that would compromise your position in any other way. This may lead to you adopting different identities or personalities, which is a topic more for the future, and so covered in Part 3. But some people already do this, typically using different names.

Choice of tools

The tool or system you choose will need to handle the kind of information you want to present, and to give you some option for presenting that information to your intended audience. This may leave many options open.

Consider social or business networking systems

Social networking services play a major part of self-presentation for many people, as well as being a means of keeping in touch with a particular social circle. These systems share so many similarities with e-portfolio systems that it is worth considering them as direct alternatives for this purpose. Presentation to others is not so much an option as a normal process in social networking systems, as they are built around the practice of people communicating about who their friends or colleagues are, what they are doing, and what their interests are.

Which services are popular will undoubtedly change over the years as the business models and fortunes of competing systems go up or down, particularly when new services offer new functionality that answers people's real needs and desires.

Other electronic non-portfolio options

The older option of a simple static website is still viable for many self-presentation purposes. The idea of a self-made e-portfolio, constructed using the generic tools that are widely available, is by several authors, taken to include people building their own website. Building your own website has advantages and disadvantages:

- Your own website is completely flexible. You can put in anything you want, and you do not have to include any content, or formatting, that you do not want, which you may have to include if you use an e-portfolio system.

- Your own website cannot automatically use information that you have gathered for other purposes, unless you happen to have been very particular in putting relevant information into web page form, in a way that it can be linked together effectively. Static web pages do not update themselves automatically, and if you have more than one version of any information, when it needs updating it will need to be updated everywhere, and that process is easy to lose track of.
- Ordinary websites offer no gradation of privacy. The content is either unpublished, in which case only you can view it, or it is published for anyone whosoever.
- It is possible to create password-protected areas of a website, but this is less straightforward and tends to need more technical expertise than simply writing web pages in the first place.
- An ordinary static website comes with no provision of support for the processes of deciding what to present.
- Writing readable and attractive pages needs a certain amount of competence, plus any expenses in connection with hosting and domain names. Do you have that competence, or would it be safer to rely on an e-portfolio or other system?
- Businesses have been keen to have their own web pages ever since the web became popular. Are you looking to present a business service or proposition?

Blogging tools offer another route to self-presentation. The assumption behind most such tools is that the blogger (the person writing the blog) wants to present themselves, so again little attention is given to gradations of privacy, and password protection may not be offered. Equally, blogging systems do not presume to offer guidance about what other people want to read. Blogs seem to have taken over from personal websites as the electronic medium of choice for presenting personal views to a general audience. This may be because blogging tools are so much easier to manage than static web pages.

Most recently, video sites like YouTube have offered an even more direct way of presenting yourself, if you think that video might be a suitable medium. As with many media, a sensible approach is to see what other people do, and judge what comes across as giving the same kind of impression that you would like to give.

E-portfolio tools

E-portfolio tools vary greatly in their capacity to support presentation to others. Portfolio tools intended as assessment management systems may allow access only to people who are playing a part in the assessment process. In such a case they would be useless as general presentation tools. Some older electronic personal development planning tools supported skills audit, but not presentation to others.

Most more recent e-portfolio tools are designed with presentation to others in mind. There are various ways of achieving different levels of privacy, and as tools are developing all the time, it is worth checking out what different systems allow. For instance, the portfolio holder may be able to send a special link by e-mail, which allows access to a specific portfolio presentation for a specific length of time; other systems only allow access to people registered on that system.

Previewing an idea from Part 3, it is possible to envisage a very rich functionality for the presentation of self. This would include something like:

- the ability to distinguish various of your own personalities;
- the assignment of personal information to one or more of your personalities;
- the creation of audience groups;
- the assignment of individuals in your audience to one or more audience groups;
- regulated permission of audience groups to access information association with your personalities.

As far as I know, however, no tool yet offers this rich functionality.

Other action points to consider

Look at other media

This chapter has assumed that you do not want to create an autobiography. However, it is worth questioning this assumption, alongside considering other electronic and non-electronic options, so that you can be clear whether an e-portfolio tool or system is what you need. Other media offer a wide range of levels of formality and commitment:

- Shop windows offer a traditional way of reaching a local audience to offer a service at little expense.
- Personal ads may reach some of a newspaper's readership at moderate expense. There tend to be some kinds of information or services that people look for through small ads, and this needs to be taken into account when assessing the viability of this as an option.
- Newspaper articles reach only newspaper readers, although articles of interest often reach people who are not necessarily actively searching for what you offer.
- Autobiographical books may work very well for self-presentation if you are famous.

Summary of relevant principles

The most important chapter to refer back to here is Chapter 3, which discusses what different people are likely to want in terms of personal information.

References and further reading

The topic of self-made portfolios using generic tools is much covered and discussed by Helen Barrett on her website (*http://www.electronicportfolios.org/*).

14

How to use tools provided for your own development

How do you think of your own development? As you are reading this book, no doubt you do have at least some ideas about the development of yourself as a person, or as an individual, whether your ideas are general and vague, or clear and detailed.

Electronic portfolio tools are often introduced or used in conjunction with such developmental processes as personal development, professional development, staff development, workforce development and employee development. All of these processes share some idea of a future goal in which more of your potential is realised, and the process may help you working towards that goal. However, just what your goal really is, and how to get there, are questions to which there is unlikely to be a simple answer. Someone with an interest in your development may have an idea of what your potential is, in terms that make sense to them, and therefore a related idea of how to help you get there. It may be a parent or teacher with an idea of an educational goal, a mentor with an idea of a career for you, or a manager with an idea of how you could be a more useful employee if you gained some extra skills or experience. But for this chapter, the assumption is that you have taken on some developmental goal as your own, and you wish to consider how to use e-portfolio tools to help you achieve that goal.

A common goal for many organised approaches to development is to gain abilities (or knowledge, skill, competence, etc.) and to document evidence for that ability. The documentation could take the form of a qualification for abilities that are more significant in the mainstream of education and work, or some other less formal certificate, or other non-certificated evidence, in cases such as hobbies.

E-portfolios are in the early stages of playing a part in assessment for qualifications. In any case, e-portfolios used for assessment have already been dealt with in previous chapters. This chapter focuses on the use of e-portfolio tools, not for qualifications, nor for assessment, but for the processes involved in development, whether personal, professional, etc.

Developmental processes can be seen as one particular kind of learning, but they also exist separately alongside learning of other kinds. Where the focus is on learning about some particular subject matter, it is e-learning tools that are more relevant. Where e-portfolio tools can be particularly helpful is in learning to learn – learning the abilities which underlie effective learning. Obviously, this learning about learning is not the same as memorising a bunch of facts about learning. It is more about the process of learning, and one way it can be demonstrated is through reflective writing, documented in a portfolio. There are various models of this kind of experiential learning, with various numbers of stages, including the three-stage 'plan-do-review' model and David Kolb's four-stage learning cycle.

As well as understanding about the process of learning, a very useful component of our personal learning ability is the awareness of our own personal general cognitive structures and concepts. George Kelly's *Personal Construct Psychology* covers ideas which I have found very useful in this area. In itself it is not especially easy to understand, but the concepts may be picked up from some of the many writers that have since referred to him.

The process of using e-portfolio tools for your own development is likely to produce records, and these records can be seen, in the light of Chapter 12, as things of personal significance – evidence perhaps – recorded for future use. This chapter also links back to the idea, in Chapter 12, that you might want to record information about yourself just to become a more reflective person. You could see this as another suitable goal for personal development.

Perspectives

The perspective here is of the individual.

In Chapter 2, the scenarios of Dawn and Leo are the most relevant. In both cases, their development efforts are prompted by advisers within their educational context, and the e-portfolio tools are provided.

Why do you want to do this?

You have been told to do it, or it is expected of you

Your educational programme, perhaps at a university, may include some personal development planning (PDP) or something with a similar name;

'academic' and 'professional' are sometimes part of the activity name. You may belong to a professional body which requires some kind of professional development as a condition of continued membership. Alternatively, your employer may have some development programme for employees, which is a required or expected part of your employment.

Your colleagues or friends are doing it

We could imagine personal development as being a trendy or fashionable thing to do, in the same sort of way as going to a gym might be. This isn't likely to be a common motivation at present, but there may come a time when this plays a larger part in motivation.

You want to develop yourself, at your own initiative

You may have an inner sense of your potential as needing to be developed into expression, or you may have ambitions which you see as requiring the development of some aspects of yourself.

Questions to think about

Who do likely tools or systems belong to?

People who own e-portfolio or related tools or systems are likely to be looking after their own perceived interests as much or more than your interests. Are you confident that they will keep your e-portfolio system available for your use throughout the period you may want it for your own development? Most likely, there will be some technical staff employed by the tool or system owner who will have the technical ability to access the information you enter about your development: are you confident that it will not be abused?

Who controls access to the information you provide?

If your contract (explicit or implicit) with the organisation that provides the portfolio tool requires you to provide them some information, then obviously they have a right to see it. They will not generally have the right to pass that information on to others without your consent. All other information that you provide should be controlled by you, within the obligations of law and considerations such as commercial confidentiality. As such, it is probably worth clarifying the various rights that others (including whoever provides the service) may claim over the information that you are going to supply.

For how long will you be able to use those tools, and what happens after that?

If you have a longer-term interest in your own development, you may want to know what guarantees there are about how long you will be able to use the same tools or systems. Personal development can be a long and complex process, so taking time to learn how to use tools to support it can be justified. If you have grown familiar with a tool that you can use easily, and it still does what you want it to do, it would be good not to have to change it.

If you will have to change tools, what guarantees are there about retaining access to your information? To ensure this, current and future tools would have to have a degree of interoperability, or there would need to be some way of transferring information between the systems.

Is the provision of privacy adequate?

Developmental processes are often tentative at first, and often you don't want to share the first tentative steps with other people, in case they may be embarrassing. At the very least, tools to support development therefore need to allow you to record materials privately, and only display things that you are happy about sharing. What assurances do you have against unauthorised access? (Compare the discussion in Chapter 7.)

What development is expected of you?

It is natural for an employer to want its employees to develop the abilities that will enable them to work more effectively or more efficiently in a present or future role, as long as they remain working for that employer. It is natural for a government, or anyone else concerned with economic growth, to want people in general to develop abilities where there is a current shortfall in the labour market. It is natural for an educational institution to want its learners to develop abilities or skills related to learning; and perhaps, less directly, to develop the kinds of abilities that are demanded at selection for the next stage in life, so that the educational institution is seen as preparing learners effectively for likely next stages. All these bodies may attempt to motivate learners to develop in appropriate ways. Some of this motivation may be in a more or less formal contract, obliging the employee or learner to participate in development processes.

Where does your obligation end and your choice begin? Considering this may clarify your motivation. The more you take on the developmental processes and tasks as your own, the more likely you are to feel engaged with or committed to them.

What development do you want to undertake?

There isn't a simple list of the kinds of personal or professional development you might want to undertake, as it is very much an individual matter. Development could perhaps be roughly classified as career-related or personal-related, although even that distinction may not be very helpful, as there could well be substantial overlap.

The process of deciding what development to undertake may itself be seen as a vital personal development task. Indeed, particularly if learning and development are seen as lifelong processes, the end of one stage, with the achievement of some developmental goals, will be the beginning of a new stage with new goals.

How much do you know about the processes you want to undertake for your own development?

The common UK definition of PDP describes it as a 'structured and supported process'. It often, or normally, needs to be structured and supported because many or most individuals need support, and would not be confident about structuring their own personal development. If you are exceptionally aware and knowledgeable, you may not need external structure and support. Most people, however, will probably want some kind of help with this. What kind of help or support do you need?

There are perhaps as many ideas about personal development as there are about education. So, if you do indeed want some help or support, you will have an interest in just what kind of support comes along with the e-portfolio system. It may be static advice, a bit like a user manual, about how to go about the processes. Even that kind of advice is frequently absent, and even when it is there, it is unlikely to suit everyone. But more likely than a static, user manual approach, are other kinds of support that may sit alongside an e-portfolio tool system, rather than being strictly part of it. One kind of support can be provided by an adviser of some kind. In an educational context, these people might (currently) be called personal tutors. In professional development, they are presently more likely to be called mentors. In the free market, people now style themselves as 'life coaches', and offer ideas for structuring and supporting development processes. A second kind of support is provided by something like a peer network. The idea here is that people who are just a little further along the way themselves, rather than being experts, can offer valuable advice and support. If you have a number of friends or contacts who are a little ahead, they may have tried different approaches, and they can offer first-hand feedback on the ones they tried.

Neither of these approaches are strictly part of an e-portfolio system, but both can be facilitated by the same tools. Peer group support can be delivered through an e-portfolio tool or other social network, and it may be a peer group that is already familiar from other learning contexts. As with e-learning tools, so too can e-portfolio tools have a built-in role for a facilitator, to support the peer group communication.

Action points to consider

If you just want to do what is expected of you, you may only need to follow the directions and leads provided by your employer, or educational institution, for the use of any e-portfolio tools provided, together with the associated support they provide. But if you wish to do more, there are other points to consider, and you may need to consider the wider human as well as technical systems surrounding any particular e-portfolio tool.

If a provided e-portfolio system can be made to serve your own purposes, as well as the ones planned by the institution or employer, and if the support offered covers your use of it, and you are happy with the privacy and ownership issues, it makes sense to use the system provided, at least at first.

If you don't trust the system you are provided with, or you have not been given one to use, then you may want to make your own choice of system. Then, however, we must consider the question of help and support. Is there anyone you could ask on a voluntary basis to act as an adviser? Would you be able to pay anyone to do this? Is there any kind of self-organised independent user group, or can you put one together? It would be wise not to underestimate the difficulty of unsupported personal development.

Choice of tools

Following on from the preceding discussion, you will recognise that the choice of e-portfolio tool may not rest so much on the qualities of the tool itself, but on the support you can get for its use in your own development. As such, you should not let your choice be determined solely by the features and functionality of the tool.

Summary of relevant principles

Personal development came up in the examples of Dawn and Leo in Chapter 2, and, in Chapter 5, as an important purpose that can be served by e-portfolio tools. But personal development is something that is fundamentally independent of e-portfolio tools, however much they are used in practice. The most useful background principles are in Chapter 5, where you can see personal development set in the context of other purposes.

References and further reading

There is much writing on personal development in general, and it is hard to pick out any particular further reading without knowing in more detail the kind of development that is wanted. You could try just asking around, or a general web search, and many sources come up which are suitable for further reading and exploration.

One classic paper in the academic tradition that underlies much thinking, and which has been cited by many other papers, is David Kolb's 'Experiential learning: experience as the source of learning and development' (1984).

The Wilderdom Project hosts a discussion of several different experiential learning cycles (*http://www.wilderdom.com/experiential/elc/ExperientialLearningCycle.htm*).

Finally, a publication that is probably not suitable for the general reader, but which has informed a large amount of work in the half century since its publication is George Kelly's *Principles of Personal Construct Psychology* (1955).

15

How to motivate and help others to use tools

One of the continuing challenges of the e-portfolio world is getting people to use the tools. It is not a problem in cases where the individuals are already motivated for their own reasons, but we still often find cases where educators or employers decide that e-portfolio tools may be useful in the development of their people's skills relevant to education or employment, while the people who are meant to improve their skills are not yet convinced of the importance of engaging with the tools, and may not even be convinced of the merit of developing the skills themselves.

General considerations on motivation

We might divide the approaches to getting people to use e-portfolio tools into three general groups, as explored below.

Extrinsic motivation: carrots and sticks

Perhaps the crudest form of motivation is some kind of compulsion:

- You, as educator, could build in a requirement to use e-portfolio tools as a condition for passing the final assessment of your educational programme. This may be acceptable in the light of the fact that qualifications and progression are full of similar requirements. But in any case it helps if the requirements are seen as reasonable by those seeking qualification.
- You, as employer, could require employees to use e-portfolio tools as part of their contract of employment. For example, the use of e-portfolio tools could be required to support appraisal processes.

- You could make engagement with tools a condition of some other benefit that is wanted or needed.

Intrinsic motivation

There are various ways in which using such tools can be interesting, fun or intrinsically worthwhile:

- You could make the tool's interface fun to use, in terms of animation, graphics, personalisation, etc.
- You could offer services which are known to be of interest to the target users, in the same way that social networking sites do, including the ability to communicate with others in various ways.
- You could design the activities to look 'cool' in the eyes of the target user's peer group.
- You could take a 'propaganda' approach, demonstrating the likely beneficial outcomes and the difference the tools can make. For instance, you could persuade target users that e-portfolio practice will enable others to understand them better.

Demotivators to avoid

The following should be avoided:

- Any difficulty in learning how to use the system presents a barrier and makes usage less likely. This includes failing to provide useful training or manuals.
- Inappropriate branding or associations may put off users, making them think that this is not 'their' system or that it is 'uncool'.
- Doubts or worries about privacy can frighten people away from the kind of candid reflection that is most useful for learning and self-awareness.
- Uncertainty about ownership, and how the users can continue to have full access to the information later, can demotivate.

Perspectives

Educators, employers and governments may all share an interest in this topic, but it is less directly relevant to individuals. Life coaches might have an interest if they use e-portfolio tools with their clients.

In Chapter 2, none of the named individuals in the scenarios fit this perspective, but some may benefit from motivation. Avril will probably be adequately motivated already by the aim to achieve the qualification, but in all the other cases, individuals in those situations may benefit from some kind of motivation.

Why do you want to do this?

You have an interest in someone else's development

You may be a friend or relative of someone who you think might benefit from the use of portfolio tools. In this case, you probably won't be in a position to decide which tool to use, but you may be able to help motivate your friend or relative to use what is available.

You have an interest in education

You may be concerned with the personal development of learners as reflective practitioners. You may want to help learners to learn more effectively. You may want to help learners towards suitable employment.

You have an interest in employment

You may be concerned with employee development, either because you want to be a good employer, concerned with the interests of your employees for their own sake (or similarly, you may be part of a trade union or worker cooperative), or because you want a more sophisticated and effective approach to improving employees' abilities at work, motivation for work, or satisfaction with work.

You have an interest in government policy

You need to propose some government or agency action which will result in more people using e-portfolio tools, perhaps as a route to taking responsibility for their own learning and development.

Questions to think about

In whose interests is using the e-portfolio tool or system?

Part of the task of motivating people to use the system will be identifying any interests of theirs that it supports. Much of this is covered in earlier chapters.

For employers trying to motivate employees, it may be more effective to be open about the benefits to the business that come through employee development. This is particularly the case when employees are ready to see their interests aligned with those of the business, perhaps because of job security. However, in a culture where labour relations are problematic, and the view is that employer interests are naturally opposed to employee interests (perhaps as represented by trade unions), motivation by appealing to the interests of the business could be less effective. In this case it would be essential to collaborate with trade unions in the introduction of e-portfolio tools, or even just delegate the whole matter to trade unions.

Similarly, for educational institutions there is the question of how much the institution really focuses on the interests of the students, and how much it is able to admit to organisational necessities and interests. The way of presenting institutional interests to students may also depend on their attitude to the institution. Do they have a sense of pride in belonging, or is the institution simply seen as a convenient way to get a qualification? Or worse, is the institution seen as setting petty conditions and restrictions on their enjoying student life, and their 'natural' right to get a qualification at the end? An extra challenge here is that you may have a mix of students with different attitudes. Are you able to personalise your provision of development according to the attitude of the student? This would be very advanced, and challenging, but might be correspondingly worthwhile if the challenge can be met.

For motivation in general, it is probably safest to focus on the interests of the individual – most easily on their direct selfish interests, but also possibly on their 'enlightened' broader interests. This will only be honestly possible if the e-portfolio system is indeed designed to support the interests of the individual users.

How much privacy and security are required?

In essence, how sensitive are the users likely to feel about the possibility of various kinds of information being seen by others, who they have not specifically permitted? The more users are concerned about this issue (whether rightly or wrongly), the more effort will have to be made to convince them of the privacy and security of the system.

How are various kinds of e-portfolio system perceived by users?

It can be quite a challenge, for anyone, to look beyond their own perspective, and to include the perspectives of others. Because computer and information systems have had to tackle this issue many times in the past, it is familiar in the fields known as 'systems analysis' and 'systems development methodology'. Getting it wrong can be easy and costly. Some of the most influential approaches to this challenge originated in the 1970s or even earlier. Approaches include the Socio-Technical Systems approach, pioneered by the late Enid Mumford, and the Soft Systems Methodology of Peter Checkland.

Soft Systems Methodology, in particular, is designed to help the systems analyst clarify the perspectives of the multiple stakeholders in the development of an information system. My personal view of the essence of the Soft Systems approach is that it guides the systems analyst to plan systems developments that make good sense to all stakeholders, even where different stakeholders understand the same system in different ways. The development stands a better chance of being accepted in practice if each stakeholder group has its own positive understanding of the role of the information system.

One of the Soft Systems techniques is the 'rich picture'. Stakeholder representatives compose free-format collages of words, sketches, diagrams etc. to express their view about the essential characteristics of the system under consideration, in human as well as technical terms. This kind of technique in particular could help to elucidate e-portfolio users' points of view.

Action points to consider

Investigating the views of potential users

The views of potential users could be sought through informal discussion, structured interviews, focus groups, questionnaires or other surveys. Using a Soft Systems approach to analysis would lead to stakeholders developing 'rich pictures' of how they see such a system. This could easily lead to discussions with users regarding their motivation and priorities.

Motivation and persuasion

Motivating factors have been introduced above. Ways to motivate users need to be considered, chosen and put into practice. It is probably best to work with positive and intrinsic motivation. If you have to resort to some kind of compulsion, it needs to be seen as reasonable by those who have to comply.

Lead by example – use the system

It is surprisingly common to find that the educators who promote personal development planning tools to their students don't use these tools themselves. This inevitably sends mixed messages and can be demotivating for students. A similar criticism could be made of managers recommending systems to the people they manage, but not using them themselves. It is better to put in a system which is useful for and used by everyone.

One of the issues here is that e-portfolio enthusiasts among educational staff have often been relatively isolated. While they can offer help and motivation to the learners for which they are responsible, there may be no one to offer them similar support and encouragement, even if they had the time to spare. This suggests that e-portfolio use needs to start from the top of the organisation in order to be accepted throughout, and there are many challenges to surmount to achieve this.

Offer users training and support in system usage

If the methods of using the system are not self-evident, it will be necessary to offer people training and/or support. Compelling users to train runs the risk of putting them in the wrong frame of mind. Consider offering support on demand in addition or instead.

Choice of tools

People with the viewpoints represented in this chapter may well be involved in the choice or commissioning of an e-portfolio or similar system for use by people in their organisation. The decision on which e-portfolio or related systems to use can be informed by what motivates users, alongside what is feasible from other perspectives, including organisationally and technically. The overall decision may involve a complex balancing act, also taking into account other ICT systems currently used in the organisation.

It is not possible to give simple rules of thumb covering important decisions about choosing and installing an e-portfolio system across the range of situations in which they may be applicable.

Summary of relevant principles

The most important follow-back reading would be Chapter 5. The more you understand the motives and purposes of your potential users, the better position you are in to motivate and help them.

References and further reading

The following two books were influential in the development of my own thinking in the area of designing systems that actually motivate people by meeting their needs: Peter Checkland's *Systems Thinking, Systems Practice* (1981) and Enid Mumford's *Designing Human Systems for New Technology: The ETHICS Method* (1983), available at: *http://www.enid.u-net.com/C1book1.htm*.

16

How to develop e-portfolio tools

How to develop software in general is the subject of many books and courses on software development. This chapter does not attempt to substitute for these, but rather does two things. First, it gives some outline considerations for e-portfolio developers to take into account during the development process, and second, it offers an insight for non-developers about the general issues that need to be considered.

Perspectives

The main perspective here is of the person who is managing the development of portfolio tools. Consideration of the issues in this chapter will also be useful if you are a manager who has to report on the issues, to inform an executive decision about whether to develop a new tool, or if you are a practitioner who knows a bit about tools and you are thinking of developing a simple or prototype system.

The scenarios in Chapter 2 are not directly relevant, but may be useful as examples of potential users – you might consider whether your tools are likely to work for them. You may want to develop other sketches of the people you envisage using your system, and the scenarios in which your system may be used.

Why do you want to do this?

Your organisation has decided to develop an e-portfolio tool

You are a developer, and your organisation has asked you to develop an e-portfolio tool, or manage its development. This may be as a result of a decision about the need for such a tool in the organisation which is not met by using an existing tool, or it may be as part of a project which is funded to develop a prototype.

You are in the business of developing and selling e-portfolio tools

You have identified a market for some e-portfolio related tools. You may already be in this market, or you may want to enter it. You now want to develop a better tool for the market you have identified.

Questions to think about

Requirements questions

This first group of questions is intended to address the actual requirements for a system. You can ask these whether or not you have made a firm decision to develop your own system.

Who are the stakeholders in the systems you intend to develop?

Approaches like Checkland's Soft Systems Methodology help with this kind of analysis. Development of an e-portfolio system cannot be done well simply on the basis of some imagined technical requirements. A successful e-portfolio system will be one where individual users are deeply involved, and this involvement may result in them feeling strongly about what they require of the system. The success of this kind of development depends on meeting the needs and wants of the various stakeholders. You will want to do this intentionally, not just by accident.

How much do you know about the intended users?

What are their needs, and their motives? The more you know, the more that knowledge should help with various design decisions. In general terms, the kinds of people that are likely to use e-portfolio tools have been described in previous chapters. Beyond this, it is an advantage to know as much as you can about the particular kinds of situations in which they may find themselves.

For what purposes is a tool required?

Beyond what has already been said in previous chapters, particularly Chapter 5, there is no more to be said here.

What information is likely to be stored, at least by design?

Chapter 6 provides the discussion to clarify this.

What functionality is needed?

Again, the topic has been broached earlier, and it is a matter of revisiting the considerations (in Chapter 9) and making decisions.

What usability and accessibility requirements are there?

As with any other software development, there are always usability and accessibility requirements to take into consideration. It is worth considering whether the intended users have any particular requirements in this area which may or may not be met by existing systems.

What about interoperability?

You will need to take some clear decisions here. The issues have been introduced in Chapter 7, and will be detailed further in Chapter 18. There are three broad positions you could take:

- you do not want your system to interoperate, and you will try to design out any reasons for people to want to interoperate with any other system;
- you do not see a present need for interoperability, but want to keep your options open for the future;
- you would like to be at the forefront of interoperability, as you see it as important for your users.

The actions to take are discussed shortly below in this chapter.

Decision questions

Having reviewed the requirements, you are in a better position to make the important decision: adapt or develop.

Is what is needed already available within the organisation?

If it is, you may not need to go through the challenging task of developing a system from scratch. It may be that some or all of your requirements can be met by other existing systems. For instance, if your organisation has an e-learning system (or learning management system or virtual learning environment), it may be possible to use it for the educational and guidance parts of what you need, at the very least. Equally, a student records system might be good enough to hold quite a bit of the information that you want to store, assuming the students can have access to the information.

On the other hand, you might well conclude that existing systems are fundamentally inappropriate for e-portfolio use. Current opinion seems to be that students have a sense of their own records about themselves as being separate from their institution's records about them, and they might therefore be unwilling to place information they see as their own on a system which they see as institutionally focused.

If the existing systems of your institution or organisation can cover some, but not all, of your requirements, you are left with a difficult dilemma. On the one hand, you can work with existing systems, and get them to interoperate with the system you develop to cover the unmet requirements. This would need particular attention to coordination of the systems, as discussed in the following chapter. On the other hand, you can try to ignore the existing systems as much as possible, and build a separate e-portfolio system. However, this presents the risk of having inconsistent information on different systems.

Are suitable or similar services available free?

Free or open source software is definitely a possibility in the area of e-portfolio tools. The issues are discussed briefly in the introduction to Part 2.

Another possibility is that existing web-based services, as provided free by, say, Google or Yahoo!, can cover at least some of what is needed. The idea of using blog systems has come up often. The decision here is quite complex, but generally speaking, if the importance of meeting your needs has already brought you to consider building your own system, then it is risky to rely on a free service to meet these needs. Of course, if for some reason you need a system, whatever it is, and have no budget to buy or develop one, free web-based services may be the only option.

Are you sure that you really want to develop a tool yourself?

It is in many ways safer, although perhaps less exciting, to use someone else's tools than to develop your own. You need to be certain that developing your own is a good idea before proceeding. Someone with an amateur or hobbyist approach may be tempted to try building an e-portfolio system, disregarding the time spent, on the grounds that it is fun or will provide experience. If you can get external funding for developing a new system (perhaps from a funding agency that doesn't yet have a very sophisticated view of the issues) you may also be tempted to build your own. However, there is no reason for supposing that a low development cost will in practice lead to a successful tool.

Development questions

Apart from the choice of development methodology, there are a couple of other questions that can help guide development.

What about intellectual property?

Non-commercial organisations in particular have difficulty with the question of intellectual property. In essence, you need to make sure that you are allowed to do what you want to do in the future, and that those who you don't want to do things are not allowed to. So, for instance, you might want to be sure that you can modify and distribute copies of the software you have built. Whether you want to be paid for this is a crucial factor in determining what needs to be done. Another matter is whether you want to allow others to use or build on your work.

What about maintenance?

Maintenance is also not always treated fully in discussions of systems development. One of the major reasons for opting to use someone else's system is that they bear the responsibility for maintenance. If you build your own system and you want to fix bugs, respond to ongoing feedback, etc., you will need to maintain the software, and this requires resources.

Electronic Portfolios

Action points to consider

If you are building a whole e-portfolio system, then in addition to following whatever systems development method you have adopted, you will likely want to take account of the issues described below.

Security

Almost by definition, an e-portfolio system deals with personal information, and this might sometimes include sensitive information. It is vital for user confidence to ensure that personal information is only seen by others who play an essential role for the portfolio holder, or who are explicitly authorised by the holder. Ensuring this is not easy. This is a large topic in its own right, so no details will be explored here, only the briefest outline of some important points.

To be effective as a presentational tool, an e-portfolio system needs to allow portfolio holders to make selections of things (information or artefacts) to be viewed by other people, and to allow holders to select the people, groups of people or types of people that can view them. It is also very useful if the system can store a time interval for each permission, so that the holder does not have to remember to go back into the system to cancel a permission after it is no longer needed. There then needs to be some kind of security infrastructure or architecture that authenticates other people, connecting them to the permissions that the holder assigns to them for viewing selections of portfolio information.

There are many possible ways of storing permission information, but whichever way is chosen, it should be easy for the portfolio holder to review who is allowed to see any particular piece of information, and what any person or group is allowed to see.

Usability

Not all systems development approaches give a high priority to usability. If you are developing an e-portfolio system, you will need to give it a high priority, because the success of the system will depend centrally on its usability. It is not enough to give users a thick manual or offer them hours of training. Usability has been discussed at great length over many years, and although there are no magic formulae, there are some general principles:

- Have the user perspective in mind – earlier chapters in this book can be read or re-read from a user perspective.
- Involve real users in the design of the system, and listen carefully to what they say about their needs and wants.
- Have real users test prototypes in realistic situations, and gather feedback from that testing in an organised way, so that it can be acted on effectively.

Systems must be usable in the context in which they are actually going to be used. While we may perhaps have an image of a learner sitting down in a quiet room with a computer, reflecting and writing, this may not be the real situation, and if it isn't, the usability design needs to take that into account.

Accessibility

Much of what can be said on usability can also be said for accessibility. If the e-portfolio tool is to be offered as a service to many people, it is essential to ensure that none of them are discriminated against because of any disability.

Interoperability

This whole issue is highly significant in the longer term, but may not be immediately obvious, so Chapter 18 will examine it in more detail. The issues in general have been introduced in Chapter 7. Here, just a few words addressed to developers will suffice.

Initially, the most important thing for a developer to ensure is that the information model used in your system is compatible with the information model used in other systems with which you might want to exchange information. This is not always easy, as different developers often have different ways of representing the world. It is hoped that Chapter 6 will help you to think about the nature of portfolio information in a mature way that others will also be able to grasp, given enough thought and discussion.

A great help towards understanding the representation of information in other systems is by looking at the user interface from the point of view of a typical user. The meaning of a field, in the practical terms of interoperability, is not necessarily determined by what the designers call it, but rather what users enter into it. The more you can get to see how users of other systems interact with their systems, and how the information entered is stored, the more you will understand how you may be able to represent that information in the terms used in your own system. You will also probably need to talk to another group of people – those practitioners who help the learners with the tasks they undertake using the portfolio system.

If you have a clear view of the nature of the information itself, and how other people use and represent similar information, it will not be difficult to output portfolio information from your system using the same specifications as others use. The greater challenge will be to import information from other portfolio systems.

Summary of relevant principles

Designing a good and useful e-portfolio system is a very challenging task, and all the principles in Part 1 are relevant.

References and further reading

There are plenty of up-to-date books and materials on systems development methodology, and I won't try to recommend any particular ones. But two older, classic ones in particular have enlightened me about how to go about designing good information systems: Peter Checkland's *Systems Thinking, Systems Practice* (1981) and Enid Mumford's *Designing Human Systems for New Technology: The ETHICS Method* (1983), available at: *http://www.enid.u-net.com/C1book1.htm*.

Usability has been an interest of mine since my PhD days. The general principles were established early on, and although may now appear rather staid, they remain important. Some long-established websites that address usability include the US Government site (*http://www.usability.gov/*), Jakob Nielsen's site (*http://www.useit.com/*) and Keith Instone's site (*http://usableweb.com/*).

Intellectual property is another topic that can fail to be exciting. The law relating to it may vary between different jurisdictions. In the UK, a useful starting point is the official government site (*http://www.ipo.gov.uk/*).

For free/open source software, there are the two main organisations, with slightly different philosophies: the Free Software Foundation (*http://www.fsf.org/*) and the Open Source Initiative (*http://www.opensource.org/*).

Further reading on accessibility as discussed here can be found by searching for 'computer accessibility', 'software accessibility' or 'web accessibility'. One well-known resource and guide on web accessibility is the W3C's Web Accessibility Initiative (*http://www.w3.org/WAI/*).

17

How to coordinate e-portfolio and administrative tools

This chapter picks up the issue, originally raised in Chapter 7, of integration and harmonisation of portfolio information across the various systems and tools which help in its creation, management, use and display.

There is a strong case to be made for this kind of integration. Taking the simple issue of contact details, it is clearly undesirable to maintain separate systems that all contain similar contact information for the same individuals. They can easily get 'out of sync', and, this being the case, who knows which is the authoritative copy? You have the worry or burden of trying to keep all the different systems updated. In contrast, if the different systems are integrated effectively, there will either be just one copy of any given information, which will be shared with other systems on demand, or there will be a reliable method of passing on any changes that are made on one system to other systems, thus maintaining the integrity of the data.

When you enter information relevant to personal development, it is vital that any systems using your information use only the most up-to-date versions. Otherwise it can be a frustrating experience, just like having to do an exercise you have already done. We are probably all familiar with this kind of feeling from filling in endless apparently redundant paper forms.

Another perspective is that a system's functionality can benefit from the availability of information from other systems. For instance, rather than a personal development portfolio system having to ask learners which courses they are taking, it is better if the system can just fetch the information from the main administrative student record system. Not only is this an alternative to (needlessly) asking the student, but it has the added advantage of being quicker.

Not only could such coordination of systems save time for learners, it could save time for developers, who would not have to create or maintain extra parts of the user interface to ask for information that is already available elsewhere. Administrators can also benefit from the likely increase in the accuracy and more frequent updating of information of administrative interest.

Perspective

This chapter relates to the perspective of the administrative stakeholder – other points of view are covered elsewhere.

As in the previous chapter, the scenarios in Chapter 2 may only be relevant as examples of possible system users. However, they are not specifically designed to fit with this chapter, so you might want to create your own more suitable example users.

Why do you want to do this?

You are concerned with ICT strategy in your organisation

You are aware of some duplication of information about learners in your organisation, and recognise the motives to overcome this. As far as possible, you wish to see an ICT strategy that minimises redundant and out-of-date information, bringing all information about an individual together in a coherent way.

You want to make savings in IT-related costs

Cost savings may come in a variety of ways. You may want to minimise unnecessary development and maintenance of systems which duplicate functionality and storage. You may want to minimise time spent by staff, as well as students or employees, dealing with different systems that handle the same information in different ways.

Questions to think about

What are the various stakeholders' requirements?

Any IT system development gives a chance to align better with the real needs of the various stakeholders, with the converse threat of making things worse for one or more groups if their requirements and needs are not given proper consideration.

Is there an existing e-portfolio strategy or policy?

E-portfolio practitioners, or whatever they are called in your organisation, may already have development plans for the systems that they use. It would obviously make sense to take these into account.

How do the current administrative systems function?

Just what information is currently held on students or employees within the administrative systems? Perhaps even more significantly, what are the current procedures for accessing and updating this information? It is vital to know about these, as any coordination between systems will have to negotiate access to the various pieces of information.

What is the potential overlap?

Having reviewed the current and likely future state of e-portfolio and administrative systems, it will be possible to assess the possibilities for coordinating the systems. Any overlaps in functionality will be easy targets, as cutting down redundancy is likely to be appreciated by everyone. What overlap is there between administrative (e.g. student information, profile, etc.) and other portfolio information (e.g. personal development and reflection)? What about overlap in function?

Action points to consider

Evaluating the options

The options for coordination will most likely be specific to your organisation, because the systems that are used, and how they are used, are likely to be unique. However, some general patterns for coordination may help to illustrate the different generic approaches, which may be used in combination:

- One system may perform periodic (e.g. nightly) batch downloads to an area from which the information is picked up by other systems. This approach may be considered if the owners of one system (e.g. a student records or HR system) are not happy to allow external connections to their database.
- Changes in common information in one system are placed in a separate database from where a user on another system can authorise their incorporation into that system.
- Changes in one system are communicated automatically to another system, given appropriate authorisation.
- Redundant information is not stored at all. Each piece of information is associated with one 'home' system, and if and when that information is needed by another system, it is requested and supplied, if authorised.

Choice of interoperability specification

The last two options above will need some kind of common interoperability format. This may be designed ad hoc, but it is generally easier if a minimal number of common interoperability specifications are used. Interoperability specifications are discussed in Chapter 7, and the issues involved in making systems interoperable are treated in more depth in Chapter 18.

Choice of tools

Some e-portfolio tools will prove to be easier than others to integrate with administrative tools. If either system remains to be chosen, or is open to be changed, then it makes sense to select one that appears to be easier to coordinate with.

The easiest systems to work with are likely to be those where information can be extracted on demand in a common format suitable for the information concerned and its use, and where that common format adopts appropriate interoperability specifications. If the appropriate information cannot yet be extracted automatically, then either the original system developers will have to add that capability, or someone else will, presumably within your organisation. The software licence terms will determine whether this is allowed. If it is free or open source software under a licence such as the GNU General Public License, it will be allowed: the question then is to determine the level of resources it will take to develop the capability. There may be others who are in a similar position to you – for open source software, development costs can be shared; for commercial software, users can club together to put pressure on the original developers to extend towards more interoperability.

Summary of relevant principles

The main principles here are the nature of the information to be integrated, which is covered in Chapter 6, and the issues surrounding the information, as set out in Chapter 7, including data protection, authentication and authorisation, interoperability, and the question of centralised or distributed storage. In effect, well-coordinated e-portfolio and administrative tools act as distributed storage.

References and further reading

Information on the GNU General Public License is available on the GNU website (*http://www.gnu.org/copyleft/gpl.html*).

18

How to develop interoperability in tools

The term 'interoperability' has several possible interpretations, and before setting out to develop interoperability it is obviously necessary to understand which kind of interoperability you wish to develop.

Perhaps the most straightforward idea is like moving documents around between different word-processing software. Interoperability, or perhaps in this case more accurately, 'portability', here means that the records made in one system should be able to be exported and saved in a format that can be read in by other systems dealing with the same kinds of information. This can be achieved by ensuring that the exported data conforms to a specification that can be imported by the other system. This is fair enough for word processing, but for e-portfolio information it is not always sufficient. It is certainly useful to ensure that people can read e-portfolio information easily. If information is exported in HTML, for example, it will mean that people can at least read it with the help of any browser, which means that they will be able to copy chunks of text from it as required.

Beyond being read by someone, what really matters for portfolio information is that it can be used effectively once it has been exported from the first system and imported by the other. This idea extends beyond basic portability as it implies that information that has the same meaning should be represented in the same way. This idea might be described as 'semantic' interoperability. In practice, it would mean that two or more different systems could work with the same information. Furthermore, these 'systems' would not necessarily have to be software systems, but potentially a combination of human and technical systems.

The technical system developer is rarely in control of the ways in which the information is used. For example, information collected as diary entries cannot be expected to work as a substitute for a self-audit of a set of skills, even though both sets of information may just be pieces of text. On the other hand, where processes are comparable, it is vital to ensure that the corresponding information is represented equivalently, so that it can be placed in the equivalent slots in different systems. In these cases, you had best accept from the start that unless the two systems are the same, it will not be possible to transfer all the information to fit in perfectly with the other system. The task is not to achieve perfection; rather it is to get across as much information as is reasonably possible, placed in the most helpful place, and ready to be used or further adapted by the portfolio holder. Because you cannot control how the information is used in other systems, you must be able to understand and recognise when information is equivalent in meaning, and represent it as equivalent.

When only static files are produced and stored, as per the more straightforward ideas above, the situation is not unlike when the portfolio holder copies in information from elsewhere. Indeed, the decision to upload information that has been previously saved elsewhere rests with the portfolio holder. However, when systems work together 'synchronously', information may be passed from one system to another without the direct intervention of the portfolio holder. This requires a deeper level of technical interoperability. There may not be a step at which the portfolio holder can intervene to give a human decision about whether or not information is suitable, and thus the system and the system developers have a greater responsibility to ensure that mistakes are minimised. In this case, you either need to ensure that information has just one home (see the arguments in the previous chapter) or, if the information is duplicated, ensure that it has exactly the same meaning in both systems.

Perspective

Whoever he or she works for, the main perspective here is that of the e-portfolio system developer. A secondary perspective is that of the software developer's manager, who needs to know what is involved, and how to allocate resources.

Why do you want to do this?

You have been asked to make your system interoperable with another system

The request can come as a result of various motives, but the motives will probably not affect the developer's task.

You are a manager or developer working with a responsible vendor or institution

You may be in a position to make a decision about whether to develop interoperability. Considerations in this chapter will help you to make a decision about how feasible this development may be, and what approach to take.

Questions to think about

What exactly is the need for interoperability?

It is useful to document the scenarios in which interoperability would be helpful for the users of your system. What will be able to happen that could not happen before, and how will this happen?

Associated with this, it is good to consider the benefits of the proposed interoperability. If it is a saving of time or effort, then how much is likely to be saved? If it is a reduction in errors, what are the consequences of those errors? If new activities become possible, what is the value of those new activities?

Then, in terms of the types of interoperability described above, what kind of interoperability is appropriate? Is it, on the one hand, just the ability to export and import to and from files which may be held on storage devices or e-mailed as attachments, or is it on the other hand some concurrent interoperability that needs a service-oriented approach? Or is it something else?

What kind of interoperability specification is needed?

In Chapter 7, when discussing the interoperability of information, I gave a brief sketch of the current portfolio interoperability situation. I won't repeat that here.

In general, you will need an interoperability specification that allows things with different meanings and uses to be distinguished, while making it easy for information that plays the same role in different systems to be represented in just the same manner. As such, the specification you choose needs to fit the information you need to represent. But it also needs to fit the information that is needed by the other systems with which you want to interoperate.

If a specification is sufficiently modular, it should not be a problem if there is more scope in the specification than you need – perhaps it covers what other people need but you do not. However, you do not want a specification that imposes all kinds of structures that you don't need, or that is unnecessarily complex, making it harder to understand and implement.

Of course, you want to use a specification that other people use, or are prepared to use. And you may be able to influence what others use. If you adopt a specification for good reasons, and make those reasons clear to others, they might be more ready to adopt the same one. Although it doesn't always come down to this, it should be a simple matter of the best reasons winning out, for a particular set of applications, or a particular domain, or a particular industry.

To transfer all of a portfolio holder's records from one system to another, the specification used needs to be designed specifically for portfolio information. You may not need to specify how transfers are to take place, beyond allowing the export and import of files. But for the transfer of small pieces of information between systems operating concurrently, you will need to specify the services to be used – most likely web services – and there may be other more widely accepted specifications that deal with the limited information you need to transfer.

Action points to consider

Document your requirements and scenarios

This follows directly from the above question regarding the need for interoperability.

Understand the essential nature of portfolio information

This is covered in Chapter 6. You will need to be clear about how the information in your system can be represented in terms of that discussion.

Understand the role that portfolio information plays in the systems

Following the above discussion, it is really useful to know as much as you can about how the information that you have in your system might be used in practice in other systems, as well as your own. Sometimes developers may be asked to develop systems where they are not familiar with the underlying practice. The more you understand about the practice, the better.

Review the possible specifications

After considering the questions above, there may not be a great choice. Indeed, it may be quite obvious what to use. But in any case, you can take the opportunity, if you have not already, to consider how information in your portfolio system will map into any possible interoperability specification.

In addition, you might want to consider seriously the possibility that if there is a good, widely adopted specification, it may be worth modifying the way that your system holds information to make it map more easily to this specification. A possibility here is that you unpack some of the more complex structures in your system into a set of related portfolio items in terms of the specification. This makes sense because it is likely that other systems have different complex structures, which might be made out of broadly similar components. The more that different systems agree on the components, and the more those agreed components are reflected in the interoperability specification, the more scope there is for effective transfer of information, even where the larger structures and their related practice are not the same.

Help others to understand how your system stores portfolio information

Doing interoperability should definitely not be a solitary activity. You need to help others understand the information you hold, and they need to help you understand the information they hold. One very useful way of doing this is to create a test account on your system that fully uses the features you have, and that you can then use to export test information according to the chosen specification so that others can try importing it. You could use exactly the same approach for small-scale transfer of pieces of information by web services. It is also helpful to create a table detailing the data definitions of all the information that might be meaningfully transferred to or from another system. You may have to get over some perceived intellectual property issues here: are your data structures a valuable part of your intellectual property? Well, it's up to you to decide, but if you are secretive about your data structures, it will be much more difficult for others to understand your system, and hence harder to build interoperability between your system and theirs. In the end, you may decide that your valuable intellectual property lies elsewhere. In any case, your user interface will not be secret in any effective way, so you could take that as the basis for your 'public' data structure, and map from that to the specification.

Map your portfolio information to the chosen specification

The key to interoperability is to work out how the information held by your system is to be mapped to the common specification chosen by you and others. The way to do this may not be completely obvious. You may seek advice from someone who knows the specification better than you do, or you could just try yourself. If you try to do this yourself, you should be prepared for others to suggest alternatives. What matters in the end is not the way you personally think about it, but the way that makes common sense – the way that others can accept as a reasonable interpretation in common terms of the information you hold. So, be prepared to revise your mapping until there is consensus between you and others, or at least between you and a representative external expert.

Work out how you are going to import information in the chosen format

Before doing detailed work on exporting information you should think seriously about how you are going to import information in the chosen format. This is because importing is always going to be more challenging, and will need more consideration and revision. Once you have worked out a strategy for importing, exporting will be relatively easy. But if you take the first approach to exporting that comes into your head, before considering importing, the subtleties of importing may lead to you having to revise how you export.

Whichever approach you take, the challenge here is to be able to take any information that conforms to the chosen specification, and to place it appropriately in your system. It will be much easier to do this with particular examples than in the abstract. So look for what other people have illustrated and exported, hoping that they have followed the above advice about helping others to understand their systems. Try importing other people's information. Talk to the other parties about the results of this – if you can identify problems, it might be that they could represent their information better or that your importing process is not yet as good as it could be. With these concrete examples as a basis, you can work towards a more general algorithmic approach to dealing with incoming information.

If you like, you could imagine the final method of importing as involving a decision tree. If one particular pattern is in evidence, treat the information one way, but if another pattern is in evidence, do it a different way, etc.

If you have the chance, this may give you another opportunity to modify your information structures in line with the model implied by the common specification, if the specification also matches the information structures evident in other systems with which you may want to interoperate.

Export your portfolio information

Once you have worked out which patterns of incoming information map onto which information structures in your system, you can use that as the basis for selecting what to output in terms of the specification for a given internal information structure. Of course, you may also be guided by any best practice documentation attached to the specification.

Try exporting your test account information in the specification format, and ask others to have a look and try importing it.

Engage with others in the interoperability process

The attitude to have in mind here is that effective interoperability is necessarily a consensus process. You can't just do it alone, regardless of others. You may conform to a technical specification, but this will not be useful if others have decided to use that same specification in a different way. As such, you really need to engage with the other teams who are also trying to implement interoperability. This can be done by sending information to and fro using the chosen format; by discussing the result of each party's attempts to import files exported by others; or by using any web services set up by anyone for similar purposes. In each case, feedback on such trials must be taken seriously. Each party needs to export things in ways that preserve the most meaning when imported by others. Everyone is most familiar with what makes sense in their own system. This means the process is necessarily collaborative.

Other points

Once you have some basic interoperability with other e-portfolio systems, it will be time to think about the other, more advanced aspects of interoperability. I introduced the idea of skills definitions and frameworks, and the need for common ones, in Chapter 8, and will go on to some practical details in the very next chapter. I'll just repeat here the most important message, that for interoperability of portfolio information to work in the real world, and be processed automatically, abilities (skills, competences, etc.) that are referenced need to be referenced using the same universal identifiers, or else matching will be hit and miss. In effect, this means that you will have to develop a clear semantic structure for all the skills definitions that you use, and relate that to the equivalent skills definitions put forward by those people who have systems with which you might want to interoperate.

Summary of relevant principles

For this chapter, it is the nature of portfolio information that is the most important principle, and that is covered in Chapter 6.

19

How to publish terms for common use by tools

The chapters in this part are together intended to provide 'how to' guides to the practical challenges of implementing effective e-portfolio and related systems. The subject of this chapter may be puzzling in this context, but it is here because, even if not fully recognised by many at present, it is a vital component of the overall picture, which is why the subject was introduced in Chapter 8.

The whole interoperability edifice is built ultimately on common terms and their definitions, just as natural language and communication relies on us being able to agree what it is that we mean. A straightforward way of representing those common terms is by using the Semantic Web convention of using uniform resource identifiers (URIs) for concepts, as well as for web documents. Existing interoperability specifications, of their nature, define the concepts in their information model, and they often use (or could use) URIs as namespaces to distinguish their particular set of terms. But e-portfolio use in practice also relies on common definitions of abilities, such as the abilities acquired as a result of a course, or those needed for a job. The issues surrounding definitions of abilities have been discussed in Chapter 8; the present chapter will now discuss the practicalities surrounding the matter.

In the Semantic Web and Topic Maps communities, there are many examples of using URIs as identifiers for individual topics, concepts or resources, as distinct from using them as namespaces as just mentioned. Nevertheless, the proportion of those who have gone to the trouble of associating URIs with the concepts that they use is still only small. At the time of writing, it seems that the momentum of the Semantic Web and related initiatives are building up, and we should expect many more examples of terms and definitions associated with URIs in the near future. We should be encouraging ourselves and others to define and publish URIs for concepts, topics, and possibly even individual items of portfolio information.

Perspective

The perspective here is not that of the learner, nor of the practitioners who support learners – line managers, tutors, mentors, coaches, and the like. Of the people who have been considered before, the developer is probably the closest. But more than the developers, the present chapter is addressed to those who own the definitions of terms relevant to e-portfolio information, and to those who govern or sponsor the definition owners.

Why do you want to do this?

You are in a government agency interested in promoting transferability of skills and competences

There are a number of reasons why you could be in this situation. In pursuing an agenda calling for upskilling, it is vital that the skills fostered through education and training are the ones that are required at a later stage, typically in employment. Without clear definitions that are publicly available and frequently referred to, it is difficult to join up the worlds of academia and enterprise.

If you are in the UK, you might be approaching this with the Leitch agenda in mind, that is, the agenda named after the committee and report that brought it to public attention. Sandy Leitch's report for the UK government highlighted the need for people in employment to gain higher-level skills. One valuable step towards this would be to establish definitions of the skills that are accepted by both higher education and by employers, along similar lines as the well-established National Occupational Standards mentioned in Chapter 7 and discussed in Chapter 8. Some projects are now starting to address this.

You belong to a industry skill definition body or a standards body

You may belong to a body like one of the UK's several Sector Skills Councils, entrusted by the government with defining higher-level as well as occupational skills standards, in conjunction with industry sector representatives. Alternatively, but relatedly, you may be part of a standards body considering defining standards, or taking responsibility for definitions.

You may be a trainer or educator defining courses and curriculum goals

You may wish to define what are in general called 'educational objectives', and sometimes more specifically 'learning outcomes', which commonly refer to the particular abilities the learner is expected to have as a result of your course or educational programme. This may be because you want to, for example:

- be clear with your learners regarding what they can hope to achieve through your course;
- relate your educational goals to what is required for employment or by employers;
- achieve coherence and consistency across departments, faculties or institutions.

Questions to think about

What is it appropriate for you to define?

No one can stop you defining your own terms for your own purposes, but this by itself will not advance interoperability. For your definitions to be used by or referred to by others, they must carry some kind of weight or authority, and must be published so that others can refer to them.

Some bodies (such as the abovementioned UK Sector Skills Councils) are constituted specifically to define skills for a particular sector of economic activity, and they represent the stakeholders who are interested in the definitions. If you wish to publish definitions then this is clearly a strong position to be in. Those definitions can then be used in vocational education and training, and as the basis for vocational qualifications.

Professional bodies may similarly be in a good position to define the attributes or qualities that they see as making a good professional. Higher-education institutions can thus embed these attributes in their courses so that learners have a quicker route to gaining some recognised professional status.

People within universities often have the freedom to define their own courses of study, putting them in a good position to define the learning outcomes, or wider educational objectives, of those courses.

Bodies that examine and award school-level qualifications are in a good position to define learning outcomes or educational objectives for assessment of young people in schools, which can also be used by the schools as the basis for their curriculum.

Bodies that regulate sporting or leisure activities may have tests or examinations for learners to progress through, and again these could in principle be defined in a similar way. They might be used in schools to help define extracurricular activity.

If there is no such body for the definitions you want to propose, you may be able to collaborate with others to constitute an authority of some kind. Perhaps you could organise a group of stakeholders. Or you could do some good research, develop some very good definitions, and promote them vigorously, hoping that others will take them up.

If you do not have a position of authority, it may still be appropriate for you to publish your own definitions, but you would do better to relate them to other people's definitions. Best of all, use other people's well-regarded definitions, as suggested below. As a second best, make your own equivalent definitions, and make it clear that they are equivalent. If neither of these are possible, you can still publish your definitions, but as you will be unable to relate to equivalents, you will instead need to indicate, for example, whether your concepts stand in 'broader term' or 'narrower term' relationships with other people's concepts.

Do any existing definitions cover your ground?

There may be existing definitions that cover the area of your interest. If they are widely adopted and suitable for your purposes as well as others', the most sensible choice would probably be to adopt them. Therefore, before creating your own definitions, a good approach would be to carry out an exercise of 'due diligence' to ensure that suitable definitions do not already exist, much as people do when researching for patents.

If definitions exist, but are not widely adopted, or are not suitable for the purposes you envisage, you have a number of options. You could decide to ignore them, although this risks others thinking that you had not searched diligently enough. Or you could refer to them, explaining why you believe they are unsuitable as they are, and perhaps relate your definitions to theirs, for instance by using the Simple Knowledge Organization System (SKOS) mapping properties (see references).

Action points to consider

Decide on whether to publish your own definitions or to refer to others

The issues are discussed above: you will need to make the decision. The remaining points assume you have taken the decision to publish your own definitions.

Decide on a stable domain within which to publish

When definitions are published on the web, there is even more need than with other materials for their locations to be very stable, so that systems built to use them will not be disrupted if the definitions disappear or move. To ensure that you and other interested stakeholders continue to have the appropriate degree of control over the definitions, you need to choose a domain or think of a new domain name and some form of governance for that domain name. There needs to be good assurance that it will be possible to maintain the domain into the foreseeable future.

One of the advantages of using an established official body, or standards or specifications organisation, is that they will already have their own domain and governance procedures. You would have to check that these are appropriate.

Another technical option is to use a redirecting service. The Dublin Core definitions, for example, use the purl.org domain to ensure that even if their own domain changes, or they need to change the way in which they use their own domain, the established URIs will still resolve to the new locations where relevant information is then held.

Set up a stable URI scheme with provision for versions

There are several reasons why other people may want to rely on definitions that do not change, but at the same time, it is difficult if not impossible to fix on an unchangeable form for any particular definition. An approach to reconciling these opposites has been in place, for instance, in the World Wide Web Consortium (W3C) for a number of years.

Take the W3C's RDF primer as an example. At any time, the URL for the latest version is *http://www.w3.org/TR/rdf-primer/* while the current version at the time of writing is *http://www.w3.org/TR/2004/REC-rdf-primer-20040210/*.

For your own definitions, you will similarly have to ensure that the short URL for the latest version points to a copy of, or redirects to, the latest version. Whenever a new version is created, it must be dated from the outset; these dated versions must not be changed (perhaps except for correcting typographical or other minor errors).

Choose a suitable means for representation

There are three related issues here: the general form, or 'mime type', delivered on calling the website, and often associated with a file extension; the specification used to represent the information within that form; and the use of redirection. The references below give useful guidance on these topics. You may, for example, want to use one or more of: HTML, XHTML, RDF, IEEE RCD, SKOS, OWL.

Cross-refer to other definitions

One of the big threats to the Semantic Web, although perhaps not recognised as widely as it could be, is the fragmentation of definitions. It is easy to define your own terms, as you don't have work out what other people mean. As such, people have a natural tendency to laziness, defining their own terms without reference to others. But the Semantic Web is much more likely to take off if people get into the habit of always cross-referencing related definitions. As mentioned earlier, the SKOS mapping properties represent one option, but there may well be scope for a few other relationships to clarify your view of how your definitions relate to those of others.

Be active in engaging with the relevant communities

There are bound to be continuing developments, both of other people's definitions, and of the technology for representing and communicating them. As with so many issues, it is vital to stay on top of developments, and to be prepared to change strategy when it seems appropriate. Being engaged with the relevant communities is the most obvious way of staying in touch with developments and trends. It should alert you about what technology is coming along, and keep you informed about what other people are, or may become, able to use.

Publish so that others can most easily use

This leads on to the last point: publish (and indeed do everything about interoperability) in such a way that others can most easily use what you have published.

Summary of relevant principles

The need in principle for common definitions is set out in Chapter 8. Apart from that, the goal of publishing common terms will be helped by understanding the nature of the information connected with these definitions, and possibly also the related practices. The section on abilities in Chapter 6 is particularly relevant. Chapter 5 includes a discussion about the purposes that might relate to these definitions of ability.

References and further reading

The main UK skills agenda derives from the 2006 Leitch Review of Skills (*http://www.hm-treasury.gov.uk/leitch_review_index.htm*).

The following references give useful guidance and examples relating to linked definitions of terms, covering issues similar to the ones in this chapter.

Simple Knowledge Organization System (SKOS) mapping properties can be found on the W3C website (*http://www.w3.org/TR/skos-reference/#L1309*).

W3C has also published 'Cool URIs for the Semantic Web' (*http://www.w3.org/TR/cooluris/*), a review of linked open data (*http://esw.w3.org/topic/SweoIG/TaskForces/CommunityProjects/Linking OpenData*) and a presentation on linked data (*http://www.w3.org/2008/Talks/WWW2008-W3CTrack-LOD.pdf*).

On the subject of linked data, Chris Bizer and others have published a guide on 'How to publish linked data on the web' (*http://www4.wiwiss.fu-berlin.de/bizer/pub/LinkedDataTutorial/*)

Finally, for an example of site openly linking its data, see: *http://www.geonames.org/*.

Part 3: Future vision

This part will take forward a number of ideas, some of which have been discussed in the principles of Part 1 and the how-to guides of Part 2, towards a vision for the future. It is a more personal view than the previous parts. My intention in Part 1 was to make sense of what has happened up to now, and in Part 2 to distil out some practical advice, and both of those are supported by and related to the work done by many people in the e-portfolio field. But now, in Part 3, I am taking the discussion further, into areas where there is not yet a solid basis of shared opinion in our community. Here, I am more out on my own. I hope to be putting forward ideas that are of interest to those who are already familiar with much of the material in the previous parts.

Because I have worked, and currently work part-time, in a university, I feel the need to state here a caveat, and I may as well be as clear as I can about it. I have not written this part of the book following the values and conventions common in academic life. It is not intended for refereed publication in a journal prestigious among academics. Indeed, I would submit none of this, as it is, to any such journal. Rather, it is, quite simply, the setting out of personal vision. This part represents the way that I have come to think about issues and ideas related to e-portfolios, but crosses the ground of academic areas in which I have no training. If I were to collaborate with someone in the field of, say, sociology, we could perhaps take some of the ideas I set out here, and craft them into a form in which they would be acceptable to the academic community in its own terms. If any researchers wish to make such an offer, I would be happy to consider it!

For now, my purpose in this part of the book is to draw together ideas so that they form a whole picture where the connections are apparent and the whole makes more sense than could be made of the parts separately. This whole picture is intended to present an argument in favour of a set of potentially interwoven developments: developments in the technology allowing people to represent themselves, and learn about themselves, in relationship to other people; developments in some aspects of educational practice; and above all, developments in our understanding of personal values, their origins and growth, and how we might use information about those values. The first chapter in this part further explains this interrelated vision.

20

Notes on portfolio environments and values

The two previous tours round the e-portfolio landscape – once in Part 1 for the principles, and once in Part 2 for practical guidance – have not given a good opportunity for synthesising topics in new ways. This present chapter reflects on, and partially answers, the question: given the enormous potential of e-portfolio technology, why is it not much more widely adopted, and indeed sought after, rather than having to be pushed onto learners?

The possible social environments of assessment and presentation

The choice of term to use here has been difficult. I would be uncomfortable using the term 'social systems', as there are people who write about social systems; I don't know their work thoroughly and I come from a different starting point. I could have used 'ecosystem' and 'ecology', which give the right kind of feel, but portfolios are not part of ecosystems in the strict sense, and again, I do not start where a real ecologist would start. I hope that the term 'social environment' is not too precise, but still sufficiently suggestive to convey a little of this mixture, in that I want to talk about how different aspects of society fit together in different ways, relevant to the portfolio concept, and where portfolios, as we know them, may or may not have a place. I am discussing the way that different tools and activities are interdependent, where they often make little sense by themselves.

So I present three views here, each of which seems to me consistent in itself, but in which portfolios have a different nature and role: a society without any reliable assessment; a society where assessment is by tests that are relied on as a satisfactory basis for making decisions; and a society that goes beyond standard tests, where people build up their own stories and evidence that supports their claims to their abilities. Obviously it is this last one which is the world of e-portfolios as we know them. The three social environments can be seen as falling into a sequence of development, with the first one being the least developed, and the last the most.

A social environment without reliable assessment

To begin with, we can imagine a social environment where there is little or no reliable assessment of people's qualities and abilities. What judgments are made about people are based on appearances. This is the kind of society where racism, sexism and similar forms of discrimination flourish, and where charlatans and confidence tricksters can thrive.

Beyond surface appearances, but still without reliable objective assessments, people in this environment make judgments on the basis of undisputed facts, as well as word-of-mouth reputation. Lineage or parentage is one normally undisputed fact, and nepotism is an obvious result of using this as a major factor in decisions. Personal history is another – who you have studied under or worked with is still something that is seen as significant in some circles. Some people, for example in the areas of music and business, often state these facts publicly, indicating that they are important. It is easy to see how this can lead to practices not so different from nepotism: a high-status person that you have been associated with may put in a good word for you. But who can judge the accuracy of that good word? Favouritism can too easily become the rule. A letter of recommendation, rather than what we think of as a portfolio, is what counts. This practice remains in the form of testimonials and references, although it is usually not central to selection processes. Education (as we would recognise it) in this form of society would seem to be less important than being known by influential people, and ensuring that they are able and willing to put in that good word, or provide openings to that desirable opportunity.

Perhaps a good educational image of this social environment is the 'finishing school', where young ladies have traditionally been taught the importance of appearances. At least some corners of our society still seem to work in this way.

A social environment where testing is central

We can then imagine a somewhat more advanced social environment that predominantly uses tests or examinations for assessment. In its oldest form, testing has been with us from mythological times – aspiring heroes were put to the test, and were only revered when the tests had been passed. But in the form of competitive examination, many industrial societies have taken on this kind of supposedly meritocratic system. I think of the classic examples, in England of the 11-Plus and grammar schools, in Italy of the *concorsi* – no doubt there are many other good examples. I am told that the practice originated in imperial China.

What are the components of this second form of social environment? Typically, assessment is by examination, and it is supposedly fair and objective. The outcomes of assessment are on a simple scale: it could be pass/fail, or a relatively small number of grades. These are presented in this 'testing' society's equivalent of a portfolio. We can imagine this as a CV, listing the qualifications that are the outcome of the examinations, backed up by a dossier of certificates as evidence of the qualifications and grades. At each level in this social environment, at various stages in education and employment, people make judgments affecting other people's course through life on the basis of these grades. Occasionally, ability cannot easily be represented as a grade, and we see, for instance, traditional artists' portfolios, but this is not the norm in the testing society. Education in this kind of society consists principally in being taught to do well in examinations.

A good educational image of this form of social environment would be the 'crammer' or 'cram school' – an institution where people pay, usually for their children, just to get them a better grade in examinations. The fact that these are so familiar suggests that many parts of our society continue to work in this kind of way.

It is important to recognise that within this testing society there is no compelling case for the more advanced forms of e-portfolio technology that we can already see today. Justification of some e-portfolio practices could be made, depending on which component of the system one seeks to change or extend. If assessment relies on human witness as evidence, as currently with National Vocational Qualifications (NVQs) in England, there is a case for what have been called 'assessment management systems', often also simply called e-portfolio systems. As the practice of presenting evidence extends beyond the standard CV or application form, towards more personalised and narrative forms, there is a case for e-portfolio tools to present evidence that might be difficult, expensive or tedious to carry around or send separately to people. And as education evolves away from training to pass examinations, towards something more personalised, there is a case for e-portfolio tools that help organise the personal learner experience, and facilitate its assessment.

However, as each of these advances relies on a rather different set of functionality, it is hard to make out a case for any coherent integrated e-portfolio system. Assessment management systems may have nothing personal in them at all, and inasmuch as they are based on ticking boxes, they may not even hold any documentary evidence. Presenting evidence is not necessarily connected to organising personal learning experiences.

The e-portfolio social environment

This now leads to the question whether anything can be added to the second form of society to create a viable environment for e-portfolio systems in a society that has advanced beyond simplistic testing. In my view, the case for fully functional and integrated e-portfolio systems is based on synergy between three factors:

- educational and developmental practice centred on awareness of and reflection on personal abilities, goals and values;
- effective techniques to assess and evaluate those personal factors about people that really matter in the world;
- use of the results of assessment and evaluation in automatic matching, and of personal portfolios to present a fuller picture.

Furthermore, I suggest that the case for the e-portfolio technology that we see today, and beyond, will only really become clear when all of these are in place together. At this point people will see the environment into which e-portfolio systems fit, and getting people to adopt the technology will become much easier. Let's consider how that could happen, and what happens if one of the factors is missing.

Positively, the kind of educational and developmental practice routinely delivered to young people should make them much more aware of themselves, their characteristics, qualities and values. These can be presented, as some do now, in showcase portfolios, which can celebrate learning and achievement. Good techniques of assessment and evaluation should give results with which the individual can identify. These could be used as evidence of what is presented in portfolios; they could play a part in automatic matching; and they could be the stimulus for deliberate further personal development, beyond what is offered in compulsory education.

If the right kind of education and development is not practised, people may fail to reflect on and be aware of themselves and their qualities. This means that they may not identify with the results of any assessment or evaluation, and they may not connect with opportunities for further development. Furthermore, they will be ill-equipped to put together the kinds of rich, informative and coherent portfolio presentations that might lead to their being selected as a candidate from a shortlist. Instead, their presentations are more likely to be based on misconceived self-estimations, inadequately backed up with evidence. Given too many useless portfolio presentations, people are unlikely to base any significant aspect of assessment on them.

If the techniques of assessment and evaluation are not good enough, people will not be able to use them as guides for their own development, nor will they be accepted as evidence. They will be seen as useless for automatic matching, and people will stick with more obvious, even if ineffective, known approaches, like selection on the basis of grades in qualifications, as in the testing society. The whole portfolio approach to selection would be compromised, as portfolios would, as now, only be useful for differentiating a few people in a shortlist, which can be done in other ways.

If the assessment is good, but the results do not get used for automatic matching and selection, then why should people engage in the processes? People tend to do what is necessary to achieve what they want, and if portfolio-based processes are not central to that, they will tend not to be used. The argument for matching, rather than just selection, merits a separate chapter, which follows next.

To summarise, a new portfolio social environment needs the following components:

- education, and personal and professional development, that helps people choose wisely, and that develops qualities that really are a major factor in success in their chosen courses, jobs, etc.;
- assessment and evaluation practices that help learners and others know when they have developed those qualities that matter;
- systems that use people's values, choices and characteristics, along with the characteristics and requirements of courses and jobs, to match people and positions well enough to get good shortlists;
- e-portfolio technology able to support the related processes, and the management of the information that is produced or used by them.

These fit together, more organically than mechanically, so perhaps there is a good chance that they will be successful together.

What are personal values?

Before this chapter, I've held off discussing personal values, because there is a great deal one can understand and do with e-portfolios without needing to discuss them. But looking forwards, here in Part 3, values are becoming increasingly central to my vision of the longer-term significance of e-portfolio technology and the things that it supports. Values are not easy to discuss: people don't have a clear idea of what personal values are; those ideas they do have may be borrowed from someone else. For the sake of clarity in the rest of the book, it is important to establish a clearer idea, at least about what I mean in writing about personal values.

One of the simplest, as well as most helpful, definitions I have come across is by Michael Henderson, in the book, *Finding True North*. He writes, 'Everyone has values. Our values are our personal preferences and priorities. Values represent what is most important to us in life'. It is quite a general definition, hard to pin down analytically, and thus hard to criticise. Henderson suggests that values are not the same as ethics, morals, principles, judgments, virtues, attitudes, needs, beliefs or emotions. His book continues with many exercises to find out more about the reader's personal values.

Henderson refers to, and uses extensively, the original work of Brian Hall and Benjamin Tonna, who created the Hall-Tonna Values Inventory. This defines 125 separate values, which Henderson sets out in his book. A source closer to the original work of Hall and Tonna is the book, *Developing Human Values*, by Brian Hall and others. These values are also categorised into phases and stages of development. Hall's book defines values in the glossary:

> Values are those words in the language that carry personal meaning. This meaning carries with it a certain psychological energy that activates a person's behavior and skills. These value words correspond to concepts that are common to all language. What is regarded as good, worthwhile and important in one's life. Values are distinguished from 'good feelings' in that they are held over a significant period of time and are reflected in behavior.

My meaning is close to Brian Hall's, as I see values as most clearly demonstrated by actions. But the connection is not immediate and straightforward – associating actions with values is an act of interpretation, of construing the meaning of the actions. Values are personal, not only in that your values may be different from mine, but that the way you interpret someone's actions may be different from the way I interpret those same actions.

Picking up Henderson's definition of values as preferences and priorities, they come into play when there is a choice of possible actions. Which action you prefer reveals your values. What you prioritise over something else reveals your values. To give a very simple example, in a team context, different team members may give a different priority to the opinions and directions of a team leader. By acting deferentially, and by doing what the leader asks without questioning, you express your relatively high value for what you might call obedience or conformity in that team setting. By questioning what the leader suggests, or by criticising the leader, I am expressing my relatively low value for obedience and conformity; indeed, what I say may attempt to express the values I count as higher.

If, before speech or action, we pause to consider, rather than just following our first impulses, there are plenty of occasions in everyone's life where there are choices between possible courses of action; perhaps even more choices in what to say (or not to say) in a given situation. I suggest that these choices are significant, and that they tend to follow patterns, although the patterns are more complex than they might appear at first sight. I'll expand on this in following chapters.

So why are people not (yet) more enthusiastic about e-portfolios?

My suggestion, in essence, is that both ability and motivation are lacking. People are not brought up to be reflective and aware of themselves. When Socrates remarked on unexamined lives not being worth living, I don't suppose he was thinking that most people in his time actually examined their lives, and in that respect, not all that much seems to have changed – the ability is not generally practised. Rather, people drift from one situation to another, doing what they feel they can get away with, to avoid pain, or what their immediate feelings suggest they want, to lead to pleasure. And there is every reason for supposing they will carry on doing that until they have a real motive to do otherwise. But some people do engage with reflection, like Socrates, and these days they may engage with e-portfolio practice. Perhaps we could study them more closely, work out what is motivating them, and try to transfer that motivation to others.

Whatever people's motives for reflection and portfolio use, there are some potentially powerful motivators within the vision of the e-portfolio social environment, when people have an adequate level of awareness. Surely it is a tempting prospect to work in a place where you feel comfortable, in the sense that you are surrounded by others who share your values. And surely it is also motivating to think that one can find other people who share something of what makes you tick, for whatever purposes you both have in mind.

The next chapter looks deeper into the approaches to finding work and other people, while the later chapters get to grips with the personal awareness of values, and the development of those values.

References and further reading

There are not many books that deal intelligently with personal values. Two that relate to the little-known Hall-Tonna system are Michael Henderson's *Finding True North* (2003) and Brian P. Hall, Bruce Taylor, Janet Kalven and Larry S. Rosen's *Developing Human Values* (1991).

Other aspects of this chapter are speculative, and I would not know what to recommend as further reading.

21

Matching information for people

This chapter makes a more detailed case for the proposition that matching, not just presentation, is a natural and vital component of the e-portfolio environment, and indeed how wider applications of matching portfolio information could stimulate and motivate the uptake of e-portfolio systems that offer matching services.

The difficulties of the current employment and education markets

Finding the right course, or the right job, is often not easy. The number of courses, and kinds of courses, continues to grow, and it is hard to find all of them. The particular problem of finding all relevant courses is being addressed, but there remains an even more fundamental problem: how do you know what would be a good course to take? The greater the number of courses, the more difficult it gets to know whether any particular one is the best for you. How can you tell whether a course would benefit you, whether you would do well on it, whether it would actually help you achieve your goals, rather than simply adding to your heap of knowledge? If the course is one which is likely to be oversubscribed, how do you know what your chances are for being accepted onto the course?

For jobs, finding good opportunities may be even harder than finding good courses, as employers are sometimes reluctant to offer a job publicly when they know they will be flooded with applications, and when they have someone in mind who will probably do the job satisfactorily. At least, if a job is being advertised publicly, web-based job boards and listings make it relatively easy to find. But the situation for jobs is more competitive than for courses, as most jobs have many people who would be prepared to undertake them. How do you know whether you are the kind of person that they would want in that job? Because if you are not, you are wasting your time finding out more and applying for it, and this time could have been used to find a job better suited to you.

These unresolved issues make the process of seeking and applying for courses and jobs much more difficult and time-consuming either than we would like it to be, or than leads to a good, efficient market. Many people fail to find the best courses or the best jobs for them. Many courses and jobs fail to recruit the best-suited people. Or if they do, it is only at great cost, of time, money or both.

Having jobs advertised in public media, say in a newspaper, does not selectively target those people who are most suited. You can run your eye down the job adverts, thinking about which job would be nice to have, but you don't know whether the company or organisation offering the job would really want you. The result is that too many people apply for jobs for which they are not really suited. It would be much better if we knew what jobs we stood a reasonable chance of getting, so that we could focus our efforts accordingly. No one wants to be wasting time applying for jobs where they do not stand a chance. Equally, presentation of yourself addresses only the other side of the equation. You (as a job-seeker) set out what you have to offer, but you have to guess who might want you so that you can send or make your presentation to them. There is no easy way to integrate both sides at once.

From an employer's point of view, it is a waste of time to read applications from people who are obviously not suited. It is difficult for an employer to target the most likely candidates – this is why head-hunters are often paid a lot of money. A problem with public job adverts is that job-seekers are increasingly selective about the media they consult, as there is far too much information to take in; adverts are therefore only going to reach the people who are searching diligently. If they could target just those of us who are likely to be interested in that job offer, we would be more likely to pay attention.

Making improvements towards addressing these problems is a key aspect of e-portfolio use that will contribute to the e-portfolio society envisioned in the previous chapter.

How matching should work for education and employment

When we want a course, or need a job, we gather a lot of information relevant to ourselves, to present that information to others. We clearly believe that others will be interested. We also seek information about opportunities, or information about other people, and it is not difficult to see that, in principle, there can be a two-way matching process involving personal information.

How is this different from a plain search? If you are shopping, the goods that you shop for do not care who looks for them or finds them, and there is no need for you to supply personal information while you shop. In fact, when we shop in an open market, we rarely come across any request to supply information about ourselves. The most that would be useful would be to store information about any persistent preferences – something that good market traders do in their heads for regular customers. In this kind of situation, search is just what is needed. All the goods we might want can be virtually spread out in front of us so we can make our choices based only on our preferences.

The big difference, when we are searching for other people or for jobs, is that the other people do care about our characteristics. If we do a one-way search for jobs or other opportunities, as if they were inanimate goods to shop for, it disregards their preferences. If an employer searches through a large database of people who may want a particular job, they generally cannot know who really wants that job, and they are not taking our preferences into account.

Ideally, when we search, we want at the same time to provide information about ourselves to be considered by the other person, in the expectation that the other person cares about the information we supply. And indeed, in the cases of, for example, employment or friendship, both parties do normally care about what kind of person the other one is, and what they have to offer. Both parties have their own needs and wants on the one hand, and what they have to offer on the other. What one party wants can be compared with what the other offers. The same applies, although less formally and explicitly, in making friends.

This two-way matching process thus involves four components. For potential employment, the job-seeker has experience, competence and knowledge to offer, and wants certain terms, conditions, working environment, and of course money; the employer has the money, other terms of employment, and working conditions to offer, and wants to find someone who can do the job and will fit into the role. One service that makes this explicit is the Dutch Centrum voor Werk en Inkomen public employment service.

The technical side of matching both ways at the same time is far from the only challenge. A deeper issue is that people often do not really know what they want or need. The fact that people make so many sub-optimal choices of jobs strongly suggests that they do not know what would be a good job for them. Nor is it surprising, given that many people don't know what is good for them, that people are also unclear about what it is they have to offer that might be wanted by others.

Development for matching

To play a proper part in these two-way matching processes, e-portfolio systems need to be able to store detailed information about what we want, as well as what we have to offer. Second, they have to support the development processes that help us understand ourselves better. Our own appreciation of what we want, or what is good for us, as well as what we have to offer, can be enriched and developed. E-portfolio practice, as personal development as well as careers guidance, has to varying degrees addressed both, and this is likely to help people find better matches.

The main emphasis in personal development planning (PDP) and careers guidance has been on clarifying what we have to offer. This makes sense in a labour market dominated by employers, rather than employees. When jobs are relatively scarce, employers can ask for more information and offer less information about themselves (as well as less pay). It is therefore up to job-seekers to learn how to present themselves better, so that employers can assess their suitability from their own perspective.

The other side of the balance is to get a better idea of what is good for us, and this has not been so well developed in PDP and careers guidance practice. What suits an individual in terms of employment is potentially quite complex, going far beyond a simple level of pay. Little effort seems to be devoted to helping people understand what they themselves really want and need. It is quite challenging to help people know themselves sufficiently well so that they have a good idea about what kind of employment they will find best for themselves. Fairly commonplace in careers guidance are tests to help you identify the kind of job that might be suited to you. Some people find these helpful, others do not. But even where it is helpful, the kind of job suited to us only represents a small part of the significant differences between jobs that make a difference to us as job or career seekers. What is advertised in a job advert – pay, some outline conditions perhaps – is also a small part of what matters to people. Probably much more significant are factors like how good your managers are, and whether your colleagues form a congenial, supportive group. Another closely related question and concept relates to what the corporate culture is like. 'Life/work' or 'work-life' balance is one factor in personal satisfaction, but perhaps even more importantly there is the quality of work itself. And there is no one single corporate culture that is best for everyone. Some people like more support, some prefer more independence and responsibility. Some like a more social and friendly atmosphere at work, some prefer a more formal and unemotional environment.

Surprisingly perhaps, there seems to be little help given to people to understand their own preferences in this area. These preferences are closely related to personal values. Because it is not something that is talked about a great deal in normal socialising, we may not even be aware of what we prefer, or we may have an idealised idea of what we feel we 'should' prefer, while not knowing what actually brings out the best in us. To help with this, the ideal would be to have a wise life coach; but not all life coaches are wise, and they cost money (unless you can get a friend or relative to act in this role). But just as e-portfolio technology helps with PDP, the same technology could help in this area as well. We could envisage an e-portfolio process to help us identify when we are more or less stressed, when we perform well and when not, and what effects we can see on those around us. Some of this could be done in conjunction with a work-based appraisal system, perhaps working hand-in-hand with e-portfolio technology.

Let's go back to the employer's perspective for a moment. An employer wants to know that a prospective employee has the ability to do the job, but that is not all. The employer wants the employee to fit in with the work environment, so that there is harmony rather than disruption. And perhaps more than anything else, an employer fears something going seriously wrong, like an employee turning out to be untrustworthy, or liable to make serious errors of judgment. If that were to happen, the employer could be worse off than before, possibly having to face the task of dismissal, and recruiting someone new for the post. These issues can be addressed, up to a point, by detailed questioning on employment history ('why did you leave that job?') together with references from past employers. The difficulty here is that such detailed questions can normally only be asked at interview, and references are often only taken up after interview, when considering whether to offer the job.

As such, it would be useful if we (as prospective employees) could offer evidence of our trustworthiness, our character and our personality as well as our preferences. These things are closely linked to each other and to our personal values. At present it is difficult to make any clearly meaningful statements about our personal values, because there is no precise language to describe them, even if we are aware of what they are. Nonetheless, it is possible to envisage processes and practices, supported by e-portfolio systems, to help with developing an awareness of our personality and values, and to present evidence for these. This needs some new thinking, and merits not one, but two chapters, which follow this one.

Synergy with matching for other reasons

When discussing these two-way matching ideas, I usually find that people understand most easily if I talk about dating. All adults more or less understand what is involved in dating. Both people have characteristics and preferences, and these have to match up both ways round. And in terms of web-based services offered to the public, there is probably more money in dating than anything else except employment and shopping. In terms of matching involving e-portfolios (and considering that portfolios aren't much use for shopping), it makes sense to consider dating next after employment.

On the surface, it might seem that there is not much overlap between the information used for applying to courses and jobs, and the information used for dating. Height, build, etc. only belong to application forms for employment where physical characteristics are clearly relevant – I cannot think of a legitimate reason for having eye, hair or skin colour on a job application form. If it were indeed true that there was no significant overlap between the information used in each case, there would be little point in suggesting a common tool for jobs, study and dating. Much the same could be said of many different areas of life where we use information about ourselves and others. Apart from our contact details, which are fairly universal, the relevant 'hard' facts about ourselves tend not to overlap substantially. For educational opportunities, we have level of education completed, qualifications and grades. For employment, we have qualifications, employment history and evidenced abilities. For dating, we have gender, physical characteristics and stable preferences. For sharing cars, we have start point, end point and times of journeys. And so on. Because the softer characteristics are difficult to define and measure, and may be unreliable, they tend not to be used.

Interestingly, looking at social networking sites such as (currently) Facebook, which we use spontaneously, it is the 'soft' rather than the 'hard' information that we tend to put about ourselves. We enter information about our musical tastes, religious views, etc. We commonly take tests to compare ourselves with others, and we rate our friends. Who we know is obviously a central fact relevant to social networking. Our views on politics, our personality and the like may feature prominently. And none of this is because there is any compulsion to answer any of these questions. We may enter this information because it represents what we would like our friends to know about us, or because we want to join in an activity started by one of our friends. In addition to the information put there by us, our friends have also added all kinds of information about us. Put together, we could call the sum of this information our 'social portfolio'.

Quite a lot of this social portfolio information is of the kind which is 'sensitive', or could be used for unfair discrimination, so would be difficult for employers, or educational providers, to use, despite the fact that some employers have been reported as looking at social networking sites, to see what they can find about candidates. In order for employers to use this kind of information legitimately, it would need to be reformulated as personal value choices which are not in themselves obviously good or bad, and which are sufficiently distinct from the kinds of categories on which people are tempted to discriminate unfairly. This points again towards the importance of personal values, which will be treated more fully in the next two chapters.

Before that, let's think about other possible applications for matching. One example might be to find flatmates. Users would be young adults either in education away from home, or working, before settling into a longer-term living partnership. Surface characteristics that might be relevant to matching people for flat-sharing might include:

- cleanliness;
- sleeping and eating habits;
- patterns of work and socialising;
- similar kinds of friends;
- similar tastes in music;
- similar tastes in decoration and furnishings.

Some of these might be difficult to assess, although some could be checked through a full social networking profile. The ones that are more difficult to assess may in turn be related to personal values. Again, leaving aside values for a fuller treatment in the following chapters, we have things like habits and environmental preferences. Couldn't this kind of thing could be relevant to the workplace as well?

There could be many more of these kinds of applications where people want to associate with others, for whatever reason. Each application is likely to have its own particularly relevant information, but all applications will have an interest in those softer characteristics which help towards people getting on and trusting each other.

I suspect that the more one includes such soft information relevant to trust within an e-portfolio system that can share the information with others, the more extra uses for the information will be found. One of the basic ideas of Web 2.0 is that information that is made available as a result of one process can be fortuitously (or serendipitously?) re-purposed for use by other processes – a 'mash-up' is where information from more than one source is combined. And, as the information is put to a greater number of uses, so the motivation for people to supply that information will be greater. The same applies to information originally collected through shopping. If we were able to get easy access to our records not only at Amazon and other web shopping concerns, but also the large amount of information gathered through the use of loyalty cards in ordinary shops, we might be able to use that as extra information to help with networking or matching, as well as shopping. There might, for example, be a reason why we would want to find other people who buy the same kinds of things, particularly where the purchases are connected with a particular lifestyle, belief or set of values. Ethical consumerism has been growing for some years. This brings us back yet again to the significance of personal values.

As a footnote to this chapter, I'd like to recall the concept of a 'holistic' view of individual people. The word seems to be less fashionable than it was a few years ago, but it still implies the idea of taking into account all the different aspects of someone, rather than focusing narrowly on the information which may be assumed to be most closely related to whatever task you have in hand. A holistic approach to jobs, to dating or to other areas of life, is more likely to use information that is common and relevant to many situations, and at the same time, that is relevant to people's values, and to what they feel is at the core of their identity.

References and further reading

Centrum voor Werk en Inkomen (Centre for Work and Income) has a Dutch language website (*http://www.werk.nl/*).

22

Personal values, identity and personality

There seem to be plenty of pointers towards the potential importance of personal values in e-portfolio information. As discussed previously, people do record value-related information, for example, in social networking systems. What, then, stands in the way of that information about values being used by e-portfolio systems, for applying to educational establishments, applying for jobs, or for finding other people through matching?

The results of many psychological tests can vary depending on the situation of the person taking the test. This seems likely to be as true for personal values as it is for the 'big five' personality traits. Why and how they vary seems less clear: the answers don't seem to have reached the academic mainstream yet. My supposition is that most of us are less than fully comfortable about clearly identifying our values, because our lives call for us to display different values in different situations. We find it difficult to reconcile the awareness of this inconsistency together with the expectation that we have a self-concept or self-identity with a particular static set of values, coherent throughout our lives. To go into this further, we need to speculate a little about certain aspects of identity and personality. In this chapter I'll try to set out what I can see as going on in these aspects of our lives, and in the next chapter address the question of what we might do about it. If you like, you can see this as setting out a possible research programme.

When we talks about someone's identity, or their personality, we may be making the assumption that a normal individual human being has just one identity, and just one personality. When asked to prove your identity, you tend to produce documents such as passports or driving licences, which have your photograph, name, and perhaps other personal information. In many cases, there is an underlying assumption that there is a physical human being in the picture. This makes sense in many contexts, particularly, for example, in the context of family relationships, where genetic identity is highly significant. But when we talk about our identity, we usually mean much more than the physical and bodily aspects.

The assumption that an individual's personality is consistent across different situations is still common, although the research community seems to have moved away from this view. Commonly, when we ask what kind of person someone is, we do not specify the context. When someone says 'but in that situation, he was a different person!', we take that, with surprise, as the exception. We may take tests to reveal what we think of as our (single) personality, and the results are not normally given as 'in this situation your personality is...', but as something that is assumed to be stable. The expectation, the social norm perhaps, is that we have an integrated personality, and yet we all probably experience ourselves, as well as other people, as changeable in behaviour, rather than consistent and coherent.

Much common experience and common sense about these topics is set out by Rita Carter in her book, *Multiplicity: The New Science of Personality*. She explains well the multiplicity of people's personalities. The extreme and unusual case of incoherence is when people suffer from what is known as 'multiple personality disorder', where they have two or more separate and apparently unrelated personalities. Such a mental disorder is not directly under the control of the one who suffers it. Extending her approach to more common cases, it is easy to imagine people deliberately leading a 'double life', where they may for instance display one personality at work and a completely different one, say, in a nightclub. Then there are undercover agents, who professionally use assumed identities as well as personalities. Even more commonly, all play-acting implies that people temporarily perform as personalities and identities that are not their usual ones. The idea of normal life being like play-acting was explored by Erving Goffman, best known through his book, *The Presentation of Self in Everyday Life*, in which his approach is called 'dramaturgical'.

Though Goffman himself does not use the term, 'persona' is a word that has come to be used in conjunction either with actual drama, or with situations where people are playing roles, such as in virtual worlds. There are not yet any stable, commonly agreed terms to use in discussing these matters. Rita Carter uses the term 'personality', defining it as 'a coherent and characteristic way of seeing, thinking, feeling and behaving'. The term 'persona' is sometimes used in a more specific way, and the term 'identity' means a whole host of different things in different settings. But probably the term 'identity' is always, in some way, related to information by which people identify themselves or are identified, either as individuals or as the players of roles. If one looks up 'personal identity', 'social identity', 'personality' and 'persona', it is easy to become confused. There are no widely accepted, clear distinctions, so I will try to indicate a set of concepts that I see as being of relevance, and to suggest suitable terms for those concepts, at least so that we can discuss the ideas further in this book.

Different situations and contexts

First, I need to explain how I will use the terms 'situation' and 'context'. I think of situations as being the events and experiences that come up throughout the flux of our lives, with no two situations being exactly alike. But there are patterns in these situations, and we see them as being grouped together as kinds of situation, where we treat situations of the same kind in a similar manner. We can see the kind of situation we are in as the context for our actions, for our choices, for our behaviour, and indeed for the values that we express or display. I will therefore use the term 'context' to mean the kind or type of situation, thought of in terms of our response to situations of that type. Some of these contexts are social, in the normal sense of the word, some are solitary, where the social dimension is characterised by the absence, rather than the presence, of other people.

Some of these contexts will be familiar to many people: in a classroom, at work, at home with family, out with friends, in bed with one's partner, or alone. Different contexts call for many differences in verbal and non-verbal behaviour, in appearance, etc., in ways which are obvious, if you think of the examples given. What is socially acceptable to do, to wear, to say, varies according to context. But there are no universal rules governing this variation. Different cultures, different families, different clubs, have different rules, whether they are explicit and written (in which case they may have calculated sanctions for breaking the rules), or whether they are just conventions (where breaking the rules is met with signs of disapproval from other people, or perhaps ostracism). In response to social pressure, or being laughed at, we all feel the pressure to behave in ways that depend on the social context as defined by those around us.

However, there is a personal dimension to this. There may be social norms, but we do not all behave exactly the same in a given social context. People take time to learn the 'rules' in a new context, and until they have learned those rules, they may behave in a way which is more appropriate to some other kind of situation. Even when people have been exposed to situations of a certain kind, some conform more easily to social pressure, while others resist, and continue to behave at least partly in their own way. In the end, each person settles on their own distinctions between what they see as the contexts of their values, so that they have their own categorisation of situations that are similar or different in their view. They will then dress, appear, behave and speak, in ways that they believe reflect themselves appropriately in those kinds of situation. To repeat the point, for emphasis, this idea of context is a personal one, although the personal structure of people's contexts is influenced – more or less strongly depending on the individual – by the social norms around them.

There is a large range of difference in people's responses. Some contexts may be seen as very similar; for example, the only distinction in your behaviour between two contexts might how ready you are to speak. Other kinds of situation are perceived by us as completely different, and we would never adopt the words, dress, behaviour, etc. from one context in the other. Perhaps this is most strikingly demonstrated in our behaviour alone, where there are no other people to apply social pressure directly. The kinds of situation in which we are alone ranges from the sublime to the ridiculous, from a revered place of worship to the bathroom, and clearly our behaviour is very different, and quite probably consistently so, even though we are alone.

We sometimes make mistakes in interpreting the social situation; those who are more socially adept tend to make fewer mistakes. We may make mistakes simply because we have not learned how to behave in certain kinds of situation, or because some cue suggests a different kind of situation to us (but not to the others present). Some such cues relate to personal history. If a particular situation in the past was a source of high emotion or stress, it is easy for small cues to prompt us to think of our present situation in terms of the past, stressful one. The present and the past situation may be of different kinds, in terms of the contexts we are discussing here, and when we behave appropriately to the past situation, rather than the present one, it can come across as an error of judgment regarding the present context.

It should be clear at this point that the present discussion of contexts and kinds of situation is mainly at the level of the personal – the level of individual and social psychology – because I believe this level of treatment is most appropriate in the discussions of e-portfolio systems and practice in this book. In Chapter 24, I venture out a little more beyond the personal.

Roles

In most social contexts, we can take on a number of different roles. These are most obvious in formalised situations such as meetings. Normally, someone 'takes the chair', and is accepted by the other attendees as the person who guides the conduct of the meeting. There is also often someone who records the proceedings, or 'takes minutes'. In a football match, like many other team sports, there are the players, the referees, the coaches and the spectators, all with quite different roles. In a jury, in English law, someone has to be the foreman, and take on the clearly defined responsibilities that come with the role, including standing up and saying 'guilty' or 'not guilty'. The rest of the roles in a court of law are also clearly formalised.

In educational situations as well, there tend to be relatively fixed roles, although more experimentation has been done recently, for example with problem-based learning. Similar considerations apply to work. Sometimes work roles are clearly delineated, sometimes less so. Some people like clear, static roles, while others prefer more fluid and flexible ones. In families, too, there are roles, but they are rarely formalised, and can take different forms in different cultures. Similar-looking roles can be played by individuals with quite different characteristics, partly depending on who is prepared to take on which roles.

Who ends up taking which role in a given context can be affected by several factors, only one of which is the individual's preferences about which roles they would like to play. A useful distinction to make here is between contexts when people actively want to take on a role, and contexts when they are trying to avoid a role. For example, it is difficult for a group to have two leaders, so if there are two people who would like to be leader and only one position, there will have to be some kind of contest. On the other hand, it is difficult to force people to play a role they do not want to play. Unless they are trapped in the situation, they are inclined to walk out.

For the purpose of the present discussion, the most significant thing about roles is that playing a role involves behaving in a certain way, and this has implications in terms of the values that are expressed by that behaviour. For example, the normal social practice of being a school teacher often involves telling pupils what to do or not to do. Expressed differently, you could say that it involves persuading or cajoling pupils to take an interest in something that is good for them but might not naturally interest them. If that fits in with the way you see yourself, you are more likely to fit in with society's normal idea of a good school teacher. But if you don't like telling others what to do, or it doesn't come naturally, or you don't think it is the right way to be living, then it is going to be difficult.

The acceptable role behaviour in some contexts is highly 'scripted', so to speak: there are definite expectations about what to say and do in the situation. This can be seen, for example, in the role of a waiter in a restaurant. But for most roles, your role-playing will extend to other situations which are not scripted and you have to make up an appropriate response. This is not difficult to imagine for a waiter. If one is 'into' playing the part, then the values expressed in the scripted behaviour will carry over to the non-scripted behaviour. Indeed, the values will help you make up your eventual response and you will come across as consistent in that role. But if you do not identify with the values associated with the role, there is a real risk that in unscripted situations, your behaviour will appear inconsistent with what is expected. People may come to believe that 'your heart isn't in it', which may lead progressively to questioning your role, even in scripted situations.

Different values in different contexts

If we have to play roles so different that the values expressed in the different roles conflict, requiring incompatible behaviour, one way of coping is to develop a different personality for each role that expects different values. As the teacher, you could try taking on more normal teachers' values, and learn at least to get used to them, if not to like them, for when you are playing that role. You might still be able to retain easy-going values in other situations. I guess your experience may be similar to mine: I can think of teachers who seem to be stereotypical teachers throughout their lives, and I can think of teachers who have quite a different personality away from the classroom, although it might come as a shock to most of their pupils.

If you have a strong set of 'core' values, another common strategy is simply to avoid the kinds of situation where you are likely to be cast into a role where your behaviour will imply values in conflict with your core values. Alternatively, if you find yourself in such a situation, and feel doubtful about your ability to resist pressure to behave in accordance to the norms for such a conflicting role, you may be able to get out of that situation.

Each of these strategies has its own drawbacks. If you adopt several roles where you display different conflicting values to suit each role, there is the risk of suffering stress, or even depression, from the conflict. You could lose hold of any core values you might have been nurturing. Or you could come to be seen by others as a person of no principle, reminiscent of the satirised Vicar of Bray. This strategy, as well as being generally acknowledged as leading to less personal satisfaction, and more illness due to the increased stress, could also lead to a society in which no one can trust anyone else deeply, because everyone's values depend on the role they happen to be playing in that situation. Sidney Jourard is one author who stresses the value of self-disclosure and the danger of not being true to yourself.

If, on the other hand, you take the opposite strategy, absolutely refusing any compromise, you are liable to become ever narrower as you withdraw from any activity that conflicts with your set values. The frightening aspect of this can be seen in how we may imagine a fundamentalist terrorist mindset developing. There, a rigid set of values is put across strongly, alongside beliefs that reinforce those values, and victims may progressively withdraw from the rest of life, as everything else apart from the pure cause comes to be recognised as compromised. What is left of their lives is so empty (in ordinary terms) that suicide is relatively easy to contemplate.

With two such opposite dangers in view, it seems important – I would say, vital – for society to try to guide people away from both extremes. Understanding personal values appears highly relevant, and if e-portfolio tools can help support the kind of personal development which is appropriate to this, this kind of tool could become very significant for society as a whole.

Although this treatment of the topics is rather cursory, rooted more in a vision for e-portfolio tools than in established social psychology, I hope it is enough to form the basis of a discussion of how e-portfolio tools and practice can be significant and valuable in relation to identity, personality and personal values.

References and further reading

A new exposition that I find very helpful is Rita Carter's *Multiplicity: The New Science of Personality* (2008).

The next two books are accessible classics – I am indebted to the late Michael Argyle for, many years ago, drawing my attention to the significant contrast between the authors: Erving Goffman's *The Presentation of Self in Everyday Life* (1959) and Sidney Jourard's *The Transparent Self* (1964, 1971).

I would also recommend Michael Argyle's work as highly accessible social psychology, although not explicitly dealing with the particular issues I tackle here.

Finally, a very useful book dealing with family roles and development within the family, is Robin Skynner and John Cleese's *Families and How to Survive Them* (1983).

23

Developing personality and personal values

How personal values may develop naturally

Before considering any intervention, it is generally a good idea to understand how the processes that you are going to intervene in work naturally by themselves. As in other fields of interest, in the area of developing personal values, there seems to be little common knowledge that is obviously relevant to portfolio practice. One classic exception to this is the work published originally in 1968, by William G. Perry, in the book, *Forms of Intellectual and Ethical Development in the College Years*. As the title suggests, it deals primarily with student years – late teens or early twenties – although the scheme developed by Perry does reach back to attitudes more basic than any identified among his college students. The book plots natural development through nine stages of development, from 'basic duality' (extrapolated from his college experience), through relativism, towards developing commitment. The students that he studied, he also served as a counsellor or mentor through his university's 'Bureau of Study Counsel'. The university curricula did not contain any explicit attempt to promote the ethical development of the students, so what he reports is essentially the outcomes of a developmental process that went on simply by virtue of being a student in higher education. One notable feature of Perry's work is that the assessment of where students were in their development came from recorded interviews that reflected on their life and study over the previous year. We will return to the theme of reflection soon.

For our purposes here, I will need to go beyond Perry's work, to a simple model of how people develop over time, from childhood onwards, in terms of personality and personal values. I have put this simple model together for the occasion of this book. Perry seems not to have explicitly recognised the idea of a concurrent multiplicity of personality, and he rather stays with the idea that an individual is at one main stage at one time, although he does often notice how traces of other stages can also be present. In trying to synthesise the insights of William G. Perry and Rita Carter, I'll make multiplicity more explicit than Perry did.

A newborn infant seems to have little awareness even of different expectations of behaviour. Perhaps one of the first differences that newborn babies notice is between day and night. The difference in lighting corresponds to differences in their parents' behaviour towards them, and leads sooner or later to a difference between their day time and night time behaviour. As children grow, they slowly come to understand how different behaviour is appropriate in more and more different contexts. They notice how other family members change their behaviour, and parents reinforce this varied behaviour across varied contexts. Even then, there is still no real distinction between different personalities, nor are there real differences between sets of values. 'Good' means doing whatever parents say is the right thing to do in that context; 'naughty' is doing what they know parents don't want them to do in the context they are in. Children don't seem to have any great problem with the fact that what is naughty in one setting can be perfectly acceptable in another – many pets display the same ability.

As Helen Barrett has illustrated with portfolios created by her grandchildren, up to the age of around seven at least, if young children are proud of something, they can be proud of it in front of the whole world. This goes along with the idea that there is still a single identity – a single set of values – even though different roles have been learned. Because there is only one set of values, with one authority, this corresponds, at least roughly, with Perry's 'dualism' stages.

As children grow older, often towards or into adolescence, there is less direct supervision by parents or teachers. The school playground becomes more significant, as do other unsupervised out-of-school activities away from parents. Older children may find themselves in increasingly diverse situations that demand different behaviour, and some of that behaviour is not easily reconciled with the values they have taken on from their parents. Most children sooner or later try out behaving in ways that would not be approved of by their parents. Through involvement in different kinds of activity, some parentally approved and others not, they may come to play roles which effectively lead them to develop one or more separate personalities (in Carter's terms). In each distinct context, they will naturally develop a 'coherent and characteristic way of seeing, thinking, feeling and behaving' for that kind of situation. Involvement may be experimental and tentative, and the different personalities developed at this stage may not be fully-fledged – they may be just 'test' personalities, which may be rejected at any stage. We could see this as corresponding roughly to Perry's 'multiplicity' stages, where there is more than one authority defining right and wrong. The young person does not yet necessarily have to make choices between the value systems. The basic choice is who to 'hang out' with in free time. Each role taken on, in the context of people they hang out with, implicitly defines a set of values that tend to be learned, and then followed, in that context.

One possible sign of the young person participating in more than one value system is a new and different kind of embarrassment. At earlier stages, we can imagine embarrassment resulting simply from a mistake being made, where the right values have not been followed, and where the child is aware that they should have known better. At this later stage, with different values prevailing in different contexts, many kinds of behaviour normal in one context could well be embarrassing if displayed or revealed in another context. Thus, children may not want to talk to parents about what they did with their peers, or at least, they may give a sanitised version of what happened. Alternatively, as often reported, some young people may not be keen on revealing any academic success or effort to their peers, while being proud of it in front of their parents.

This process can gradually extend to several kinds of situation, each with its own roles, its own values and its own people. In each situation, the young person might have a different nickname, as this can help to keep the personalities separate, and to cue the expected behaviour. Particularly with the advent of the internet, where relationships are 'virtual', the number of kinds of situation with which to engage is greater, as there is no overhead of physically going to join with a group of people. Assuming one knows where and how to look, the internet offers immediate access to a massive choice of situations. It also adds several channels of communication – wikis, blogs, instant messaging, e-mail, social networking tools – and I have often heard it said that young people prefer to use one channel of communication for one kind of situation, that is, one context.

What in practice limits the number of personalities? First, I suspect that the practical and emotional effort of switching from one personality to another sets a boundary on the number of separate personalities that we accommodate. It is tiring to have to keep on changing one's clothes or one's appearance, and it is hard to slip in and out of different accents and demeanour. Most people also seem to need time, or to put in a lot of effort, to change from one set of priorities (values) to another, for example when moving between work and family contexts.

There are also processes that can be seen as leading to more coherence, consistency, or personal integrity, reducing the numbers of distinct personalities. An example of one process could be through interacting with 'close' friends. For the moment, let us take 'close' friends to mean those with whom we share life or stories in or from a number of different contexts, and contrast this with non-close friends as those who know us in one context only, who know us by only one name, to whom we show only the coherent front of one particular consistent role performance. (This definition of close friends may not fit everyone's idea accurately, but I hope it is understandable and useful.) Close friends, in my interpretation, may notice inconsistencies across our behaviour and values. If they hold some of the values we express higher than others, they might chide us for not sticking with values that they think are better. Perhaps these 'close' friends are similar to those known as 'critical friends', in that they help with our reflection.

As well as with friends, we can achieve much the same result through reflection by ourselves, although it may take more determination. We may reflect on our behaviour in different situations and, noticing that it is inconsistent, start to feel increasingly uncomfortable. The two processes are not very different, just that one happens with someone else, the other alone. There could even be a mixture of both. If you want a phrase onto which to pin this concept, try 'personal integrity reflection across contexts'.

A quite different approach to reducing the number of contexts, and making a choice between one set of values over another, could be thought of as rational or economic. If it becomes clear that people who follow certain values end up better off than others or in more enviable positions, we may decide either to adopt the values that lead to better outcomes, if that is possible in the contexts we are considering, or to seek contexts where those values can be practised more easily.

In whichever way it happens, most of us end up deciding to maintain and develop some roles, in some contexts, and to distance ourselves from others. We may distance ourselves early on, perhaps if we decide that we cannot cope with a certain role or kind of situation, or later, having participated more fully, we can distance ourselves while still keeping the knowledge of how to cope in those kinds of situations.

This is a sketchy and incomplete account of what might happen ordinarily in the development of values, but I hope it is sufficient to discuss how the processes might be supported.

Tools and practice supporting the development of values

Based on the above framework set out for the natural development and variety of values, three approaches to support seem to emerge. First, one can help people to recognise the different contexts that are the setting for different personalities, and their different personalities that have grown up within those contexts. Second, one can help people develop their personal values within the contexts in which they find themselves active. This must be done in conjunction with developing their abilities relevant to each context, and in the light of other people's values in each context. And third, one can help people reflect on their experiences, and the values adopted by their various personalities in their multiple roles, so that they can make authentic choices, either towards personal integrity, where core values permeate the different contexts of life, or towards clearer and more effective separation of personalities. Let's look at each of these in turn.

Recognising the context of values and personalities

Most people seem to have only a vague idea, if any, of their different personalities, how they work, and what values they are associated with, but this understanding seems to me a necessary foundation for the effective development of personal values. Even something as simple as reading a book (such as Rita Carter's) might help many people understand more about how their personalities, and associated values, work. Knowledgeable mentors or coaches can help where a book may not, although this kind of resource-intensive intervention costs time and money and would be unlikely in mainstream education. Our question for this book is how e-portfolio tools could make values development more practical. At present, there are no tools designed for this specific use, so I will describe what I can see is possible.

We could envisage several kinds of e-portfolio based exercise to help with understanding these basics. A first exercise is to identify the different contexts, or kinds of situation, where values are likely to differ from values in other contexts. Even without a suitable tool, you can at least go through the process of recalling and writing down similarities between the different situations that you encounter, and group these into types of situation. For each kind of situation you can write down the typical people, or the group of people involved, the clothes you wear, what preparations you make (e.g. adjusting your appearance) before going, the kinds of matters you discuss, the roles you play in that context. You may be better at this than I am, but I find it difficult to recall these things accurately. The information from my various personalities is not necessarily easily available to the personality that has sway over the processes of reflection and personal development.

The benefit of something like an e-portfolio tool is that we can record what happens near the time, and leave the organisation of that information for later. In the kind of tool I envisage, rather than writing down the significant distinctions, possibly in different words each time, you would record with the tool what has happened, probably on the same day, to ensure the best accuracy. For each category – let's take clothes as an example – the tool would invite you to choose from a list of different possibilities that you build up during the course of this exercise with the tool. Personally, I don't have many distinctions in the clothes I wear, so the list would stay relatively short. In a similar way, I would maintain and extend lists of people and groups of people. Clothing is just an example of what we could think of as a marker – perhaps not highly significant in its own right, but the kind of thing that can serve to indicate differences of context.

As an aside, if you are involved with particular activities that are worth documenting, then it may also be valuable to document the other participants' details. It may then be possible to combine this information with your contacts list, as part of your personal information management more generally. Some tools already offer some kind of integration between e-mail and address books. If this is extended to include records of meeting as well as communicating with people, it promises richer and potentially more useful records.

With these lists of possible marker differences in place – people, places, clothes, appearance, roles – categorising the experiences of each social event could be a quick and efficient process. Should something happen that doesn't fit into the established categories, then it would still be possible to add extra categories as needed. Perhaps the e-portfolio tools could offer some automatic processing of this recorded information to help group the experiences themselves into categories where particular sets of values are predominant. Alternatively, we might start out by guessing which ones fall into the same values category, and gauge the similarities on the various markers. We would probably aim primarily at capturing the more important and stable distinctions between contexts, because trying to make finer distinctions based on very few examples may not be worth the time taken.

We can then envisage a very useful by-product of these processes. Once we are comfortable with our own personal set of significant contexts, we can use these as the basis for giving permission to other people involved in those contexts. The point is that if people know us in a particular context, it makes sense for them to be able to see information about us relevant to that context. Indeed, once something is shared with one person in a particular context, it would be hard to keep it from others in that same context, simply because people in any one context tend to share information relevant to the context. So we can design e-portfolio presentations, and select other information that we have stored in our e-portfolio system, which we want to be shared with people in any one given context. This would represent a major advance in social networking systems, because it would make it much easier to present appropriate information to different people, thus presenting ourselves in an appropriate light, and avoiding embarrassment.

In addition, once we have established our significant contexts, we will be in a better position do the kind of personality tests, or other psychological tests, where the results tend to vary depending on context – this includes well-known ones like Myers-Briggs. Having spent some time thinking about a particular context, you would, when answering the questions, keep in mind the kind of situations associated with that context. It would then be possible to repeat the process for different contexts. This approach would help you to understand and clarify the personality that you adopt in different kinds of situation. The same approach would also help to focus the exercises that Rita Carter gives in her book.

Another by-product that may emerge from this process is that you may notice that certain kinds of situation or context are commonly associated with particular feelings and emotions. For example, there may be a particular kind of situation in education, or in work, where you have tended to feel inadequate, or conversely, where you have felt particularly confident. A good e-portfolio tool of the future would make it easy for you to note these emotional connections, to reflect on, to work on, to discuss with close friends, or to bring up with any advisers, mentors, helpers or other professionals.

If they were extensively noted, emotions could be used as another marker for your significant contexts. Feelings are often quietly evident in facial expressions and posture. Irrespective of the clothes you were wearing, do you have any photographs of yourself in each kind of situation? You, or your friends could look at them to help you work out what you might have been feeling at the time. Alternatively, close friends can perhaps tell you, even in the absence of photographs, what they sensed that you might have been feeling. If you have this kind of feedback, to confirm what you were feeling in different contexts, you could use the feelings themselves as a clue to the personalities that you were adopting in that context.

Having established a connection between contexts and the usual feelings in that context, you can use this to notice discrepancies. If the feeling you seem to have had in a particular situation doesn't fit the feeling that you would have expected in that present context, this could signal an inner, psychological connection with a past context, where those feelings would have been completely understandable, and where the personality you displayed in the particular recent situation may have some roots.

Developing values alongside abilities

The process described above for categorising experiences in terms of the different characteristics, such as appearance, people, etc., is quite similar to the processes already used by some tools for associating experiences with abilities. LUSID, a web-based employability skills development system, had a process of guided questions to help students to identify the skills that they had used in any experience they were recording. To help define and recognise abilities, LUSID had a pre-arranged skills framework, covering many of the common abilities which are valued for employability, but which are not often taught explicitly in higher education. Any personal development system that works in a similar way should be relatively easy to adapt for the kind of personality and personal values investigation introduced above.

The main point here is that it makes best sense to develop values alongside abilities. To take an exaggerated example for emphasis, what is the point of developing communication skills in a person who doesn't think other people are worth communicating with? Or slightly more realistically, what would be the point of developing project management skills in someone who believes that life should be infinitely flexible, and taken day by day as it comes?

Brian Hall makes a similar point: 'Behind every value is an inventory of skills. A value can only be expressed in behavior to the extent that the person has developed the skills that the value requires'. Most of the book *Developing Human Values* is made up of exercises to develop skills. This makes the link in the other direction. What good is it believing in the value of communicating with people if you lack the skills to carry out your side of that communication? What good is it to value a well-organised working life if you lack skills to organise yourself and maybe others? It is clear that what matters in practical situations is the coordination of abilities and values.

Professional ethics is one area of education that explicitly approaches the discussion of values. Most professional bodies have codes of conduct that set out the kind of behaviour generally expected from members of the profession, other than the skilled performance and underlying knowledge which are the main subjects of their education and training. Moving education in this area beyond an attempt to instil particular standards of behaviour, as certain kinds of 'moral education' have tried to do for a long time, appears to be an ongoing challenge. But trying to instil values by direct persuasion or indoctrination is neither subtle nor intelligent. If, in the classroom, an authoritative teacher tells you always to obey certain rules, what effect does that have on contexts where that teacher is not the authority, and where the teacher's values are not the dominant values? Probably, not much. In contrast, a more subtle process of support, using tools that are regarded as coming from the same place as those important and close 'critical friends', may help you to understand the different authorities and their values, and help you to come to decisions about values that really are yours.

It is particularly clear in work contexts how values differ from abilities in practice. They are complementary. In a well-functioning team, we could expect greater harmony in the team if everyone feels that the decisions made by others are good decisions. This essentially means that the preferences and priorities displayed by each team member should ideally make sense to the others, hence minimising the reasons for argument or internal conflict. If the preferences and priorities are the same, then the values are the same – at least the values that the team members have adopted for those work contexts. On the other hand, it is good for team members to have complementary, rather than equivalent, abilities or skills. If you and I were members of the same team, I might not know about the specialist knowledge that you bring to the team, so I am unlikely to have an opinion on whether you are right in terms of your specialism. However, I may well have an opinion about your actions in terms of the consequences of those actions relevant to my or our values. That's where, for team solidarity, we need to agree.

Given this close connection between values and abilities, it makes a great deal of sense to have just one tool to help in the understanding and development of both values and abilities side by side. Because skills development already uses them, e-portfolio tools are a natural choice. So long as the distinction between abilities and values is understood, and reflected in the tools, we could reasonably expect the skills and the values dimensions in the same e-portfolio tool to complement and reinforce each other.

Encouraging reflection to compare values

E-portfolio tools are relatively well-established in the support of reflection in general. Learning logs, reflective logs, personal journals, and other similar tools and practices under different names have very easily been transferred from paper to electronic form. The system, often an e-portfolio system, stores the entries at whatever level of privacy is wanted, and retrieves them for the learner to reflect on later, following whatever reflective process is supported by the tool, or encouraged by the sponsoring body. Depending on the process, this can, among other outcomes, lead to a greater awareness of the successes achieved, and challenges faced.

The processes that are supported by paper or electronic tools can be seen as parallel to the more traditional processes involving meeting and discussing a learning situation with a real person, who takes the role of mentor, adviser, supervisor or similar. It is often said that much of a counsellor's role is listening. Particularly now in the web age, it is becoming more accepted and normal for people to 'talk' to an audience that is not immediately present, so it is not really surprising that one aspect of the counsellor's role, and the role of these other helper figures, can be replaced by the blank sheet of paper, or the blank page on the computer screen, with suitable prompts to stimulate appropriate writing.

Those who call themselves life coaches usually encourage reflection, and normally discuss personal values, so one way of designing an e-portfolio system that helps with values would be to understand and reproduce the parts of a life-coaching process that do not rely vitally on having a live person there responding. On the other hand, few life coaches, or even counsellors or psychotherapists, use techniques that take the multiplicity of personality into account, and they do not seem to put across the concept that different values are called for in different contexts. Even Brian Hall and his associates, despite being in the forefront of practice with values, only principally dealt with values as they occur coherently across the different areas of a person's life. They seemed to think that anything less than a coherent display of a value implies that it is not yet fully embedded or integrated. This is a reasonable position to take, but it does not easily cater for those who have to go back and forth between different contexts that demand different values.

I suggested above, when discussing the natural development of values, that close friends, or 'critical friends', could play an important part in helping us to compare the values we demonstrate in our behaviour in different contexts, aiding what I called 'personal integrity reflection across contexts'. Taking this as a model, we could envisage an e-portfolio system prompting us to reflect on and record the different values we demonstrate, perhaps in terms of an inventory like the Hall-Tonna one, or perhaps a simpler scheme of values categories. Then, if we didn't spontaneously notice a conflict in values, the system could fulfil just a little of the role of the critical friend, by pointing out which values appeared to conflict in different contexts. 'Are you aware of this conflict?' the system could ask us. If we answered, 'yes,' the system could go on, 'What do you want to do about it?'

One option would be to reply that we understood the values conflict, and we were OK with behaving differently (we might not then use the word 'inconsistently') in the different contexts. 'You see,' we might say to the system, and other close friends who we allowed to look on, 'I have these different personalities in different contexts, and that seems to me like a good thing'. If we really want to behave in different, even inconsistent ways in different contexts, what is wrong with that? Some people use virtual worlds to legitimate different personalities expressing themselves, but what is the need for that, when there are so many contexts in the real world that would allow us to express different personalities if we chose to?

A second option would be to reply that we were indeed uncomfortable about the conflict, and hadn't decided where the 'real me' was yet. Perhaps a well-designed advice and guidance system could give us some exercises to help us reflect further on the values, the associated feelings and emotions, and the likely consequences in different situations of living out those values.

A third option would arise when we had made up our mind that one set of values was really closer to the 'true me'. The system could signpost us to resources for helping us either to change our behaviour in the context where we were unhappy about the values we were expressing, or to change our lives in such a way that we no longer needed to be in that uncomfortable context.

In all these three options so far, the reflection and action come from you alone. But as e-portfolio systems are frequently combined with tools for interaction and social networking, a fourth, and particularly interesting option would be to ask the system to put you in touch with trusted people who are in a good position to discuss the conflict. The best ones might be those who have faced similar values conflicts. This would use the matching capability that has also been discussed above. Rather than random other people in our peer group, such a system using matching technology would be linking you to others with something to offer in terms of working through common dilemmas and predicaments. Maybe you might also be able to help them similarly, and maybe those people might become valued critical friends in real life.

There is no compelling reason why any of these personal values development processes could not happen in the workplace as well, although there might have to be quite radical changes in the attitude of managers and managed alike. An ideal outcome would be that the kinds of situations encountered at work would require values that were in harmony with the core, or preferred, values of the employees working in those kinds of situation. Of course, some kinds of work naturally go along with some kinds of values, and I would envisage people with particular values moving into positions where their values fit. This would only make sense to the extent that the employees were aware of their values, but as the reward is likely to be a happier, more productive workforce, with less absenteeism and turnover, there should be enough reasons why management would want to encourage employees (including themselves) to be aware of their personal values as well as group or corporate values. They could link this to the company appraisal process, with the expectation that appraisal would be experienced as more meaningful and worthwhile.

All in all, I suggest that our personal values, and the related structure of our personalities, can not only develop spontaneously, but can also be developed deliberately, particularly with helpful tools, and together with the right people, who might also be found through the same or related tools. E-portfolio practice can help develop our personal values, which can be used in matching, which can in turn help motivate us to use the e-portfolio tools and systems with more enthusiasm.

References and further reading

Janet Strivens introduced me to William G. Perry's *Forms of Intellectual and Ethical Development in the College Years: A Scheme* (1970, 1999), and it continues to play an important role in my thinking, and I refer to it often.

Helen Barrett's website has been mentioned before (*http://electronic portfolios.org/*).

LUSID was mentioned in Chapter 8. See: Janet Strivens and Simon Grant (2000) 'Integrated web-based support for learning employability skills', available at *http://www.ifets.info/journals/3_1/strivens.html*.

Brian P. Hall, Bruce Taylor, Janet Kalven, Larry S. Rosen's *Developing Human Values* (1991) was also mentioned in Chapter 20:.

Anna and I started to explore this whole general area, in a conference paper in 2006: Simon Grant and Anna Grant (2006) 'Ethical portfolios: supporting identities and values', currently available at: (*http://www .simongrant.org/pubs/ep2006/*).

24

Ethical development and values in society

We've discussed ethical development in terms of a personal process driven by individuals recognising the values they adopt in various contexts; increasingly identifying with certain core values as consistent parts of their character, at least for the time being; and perhaps growing to shift their core values gradually as they mature and their attitude to life changes. But ethics is not just about individuals making their own value judgments. It involves others, and society, in various ways. Certainly, ethical development has to be about personal values, but we also need to think about what is good for the wider society, not just the individual. Of course, not everyone agrees on what is good for society, so the views expressed here are personal. And because this book is focused on e-portfolio technology, the issue is how the technology could directly or indirectly support processes and lead to changes that are beneficial for society, rather than what good changes might be achieved through other means.

Here, I identify some practices that may lead to change, and interweave this with a brief discussion of what may be possible.

Values tourism

Travel has been valued since at least the time of the 'Grand Tour' – the voyage undertaken by young English gentlemen in the seventeenth and eighteenth centuries – partly as a way to see different cultures and their values. You have to try harder and travel further these days. You could do this as a tourist, but if you were to become a social anthropologist you might have a more powerful experience along the same lines. Either way, the simple fact of seeing cultures with different values helps you to recognise the values of your own culture, and to put them in perspective as less than absolute. In addition, seeing the effect of these values on people's behaviour and their quality of life, opens the door to comparisons, with the result that you do not necessarily think your own culture is best.

Those who are not ready for that experience may regard others with different values as 'barbarian' or 'savage'. People who unquestioningly and unshakably hold that their own values are 'right' (as in Perry's dualism) may even be liable to think that others who don't hold the same values are less than human.

How do we help less mature people grow to that stage of accepting 'otherness' as fully human, and accepting different values as not necessarily wrong? I think there is much more work to do, to establish, for example, whether there is a youngest age or stage of development at which this is possible, and how that development can be nurtured. As solutions are found to this, there is the real possibility of being able to help with some social problems.

If the world progressed towards more diversity in culture and values, we can imagine that different groups, living with different values, would like to recruit new people who would fit in with them. Meanwhile, people who felt uncomfortable about the values they were brought up with might want to try out different cultures, possibly leading to migration to a place where their preferred values were common. I could envisage e-portfolio based processes where people explored their values, and were tested to see if they were ready to try living in a different culture, perhaps with the help of some real one-to-one interaction with a member of the more attractive culture.

There have always been tales of people 'going native' – the example that comes to my mind is the film, *Dances with Wolves* – and they vary in their credibility. But the best chance I can imagine for really being able to make a move from one culture to another is by way of a thorough exploration of one's own values, and the values of other cultures, aided by the kind of tools discussed in this book. If it were to prove a successful approach, it would pave the way for much more cultural diversity, and possibly lead to many more people being considerably happier.

In the work setting, one can see the same kind of principle working, though in a more restricted way. There must be less diversity between workplaces within the same culture than between our culture as a whole and other cultures. But the same principle, of exploring one's own values, and the values of workplaces, could in principle lead to constructive and beneficial moves between employers, or even between the divisions of a large employer.

The small group

Logically, there are two opposite approaches to the same goal of changing common people's values in society, and therefore changing society itself: top-down and bottom-up. The more famous historical, political or military solutions we can see as the top-down ones. Leaders win over the powerful people in society, take over the media, and promote their own view by propaganda and enforcing conformity. We probably all share in deploring dictators, although we may be more ambivalent about charismatic, benevolent leader figures.

The opposite approach, bottom-up, is based on the recognition that it is the people closest to you who have the most effect on your behaviour, and thus the values practised when you are with those people. Those people, in turn, are usually influenced in everyday social life by the norms in our society, and in work life by the corporate culture. The leaders in setting the norms of work culture may be founders of companies, or those who currently have power in the organisation. For any bottom-up changes to work in this model, the group of people closest to you need to interact with each other, treating each other in a different way, and agreeing (explicitly or implicitly) to behave in each other's company according to the values they prefer, not the values of their surrounding culture. How can this get started? How do people who share the same values get together, when those values differ from the mainstream?

One way of doing this is to clearly flag something about yourself that others will recognise as related to particular values, so that others sharing those values can find you and keep your company. Non-dominant religious groups, as well as many other non-religious groups, often have symbols they can use for this. This may well result in people getting together with others who share non-dominant values, but the values of the group that gets together in this way cannot be freely chosen or changed easily, as they are likely to be attached to the values associated with the larger group, to whom the symbols belong.

Thus, for instance, a house church could potentially be an influence for change in the values practised by its members, but equally it could be a means of spreading a predefined set of values belonging to the wider church or denomination to which it owes allegiance. Alternatively, to take a non-religious example, co-counselling (or 're-evaluation counselling') provides a one-to-one peer setting that allows new values in place of some normal social conventions. However, it is not intended that 'anything goes', and there are training courses that no doubt convey what behaviour is appropriate, and thus which values are seen as good.

Despite any obstacles, small groups can certainly change people's behaviour. To take a relatively recent example, the initiative known as 'Circles of Support & Accountability', in which sex offenders meet regularly with a small group of volunteers, has been shown to reduce greatly the chances of their reoffending. If a sex offender met with another group of people in just another social setting, rather than one of these circles, the offender would not reveal their offending personality. However, the people in the circles know of the offending, and meetings presumably call for review of and reflection on the context of the offences in particular, thus involving a very different personality, with socially unacceptable and personally highly damaging values. So, in terms of the analysis in this book, these circles place the offender in one context and require the offender to reflect on the offending personality in the alternative contexts where offences take place. Perhaps these offenders need the trusted small group to act as the reflector and the connector of their personalities. A similar effect may happen to us just by ourselves, when we face up to some horrible realisation, and think, 'Oh no! What have I done!'

Could there be more spontaneous house groups or small social groups, unaffiliated to larger organisations with strong values? I think there could be, but for them to form and work there would have to be a way of getting over the dominance of the values and social conventions that tend to govern people meeting others they don't know. Perhaps the breakthrough could be through a matching process, based on e-portfolio information, to bring people together based on the set of values they had been considering or trying out and recording in their e-portfolio tools. It would depend on an effective system for classifying values and helping people recognise and explore them; but if this worked, it could result in far more diversity than is currently provided by the usual clubs and societies, which are often run by people with much invested in the values that they want to see continuing to be associated with their organisation.

Values and trust

Alongside personal values, trust is another issue that recurs in the discussions in this part of the book. It is plausible to suppose that we trust others when we believe our values are similar to theirs. This is because, following this idea of values reflecting choices, those who share the same values are likely to make similar choices to ours, or at least, choices which we understand and respect, faced with similar situations involving choosing or prioritising.

The processes of gaining and losing trust have both social and psychological dimensions. In our society, the expected way of people responding to strangers seems to be based on caution and withholding trust. It is expected to take a long time to develop trust, and those who show too much trust too early are considered naïve. It is also considered normal that once someone has betrayed our trust, we find it very difficult indeed to restore any trust in that person. This must also be rooted in psychological mechanisms which we cannot dismiss or avoid.

In a culture where people tend to conform strongly to just one set of social norms, it is easy for deviants to be spotted and ostracised. The result is that people can be relatively trusting of other socially accepted people as it would be obvious if someone had been ostracised. This may look and feel comfortable, cosy even, but the cost is that diversity is more difficult. If we want to have trust, within a pluralist society where diversity is encouraged, we must adopt a different approach.

If e-portfolio technology were built up in the ways suggested in this part of the book – to help us understand our personal values, and to represent those values to others – it is then not difficult to envisage an e-portfolio tool being used to provide evidence of our adhering to the kind of standards of behaviour that promote trust, at least for the audience that we want to reach. There is an analogy to skilled performance and knowledge. In work settings, employers look for skilled performance of tasks, supported by appropriate knowledge. Analogously, what we look for, to promote trust, is adhering to standards of behaviour, supported by appropriate personal values. Just as you may have to present different evidence for skills to different potential employers for different opportunities, you may also have to show different standards of behaviour, backed up by other evidence of appropriate values, to be trusted by different groups of people, or in different cultures.

More difficult problems

The impression I get today in Britain, where I currently live, is that young people have plenty of opportunity to engage in different contexts where different values are expected, and where they can develop different personalities. The negative side of this is that there seems to be a lack of security, reflection and integration.

The mere fact that different authorities with different value systems can exist in our society seems good to me, provided that the people in our society are ready and equipped to make good use of that variety, rather than it being used as the basis for discrimination. Positively, a variety of authorities with different values can allow people to try out different personalities and values, on their way towards authentic choice of their own values. This variety of values is part of the essence of being a pluralist society. Opinion leaders seem to agree that pluralism is either good or inevitable. But what if young people are ill-equipped to deal with this pluralism?

Perry's definition of multiplicity, in the glossary at the back of his book, may be helpful:

> A plurality of 'answers', points of view, or evaluations, with reference to similar topics or problems. The plurality is perceived as an aggregate of discretes without internal structure or external relation, in the sense, 'Anyone has a right to his own opinion,' with the implication that no judgments among opinions can be made.

Thinking in Perry's terms, people who are not ready to cope with a multiplicity of authorities may either stay with the authority they know, interpreting other purported authorities as just plain wrong, or may choose an apparently stronger authority, if that suits their interests. Perry's multiplicity contrasts slightly with his 'relativism', which is more structured into frames of reference. Perry has four kinds of what he calls 'retreat' from relativism and on his chart, they are given thus:

- *Reaction*: High anxiety, complaint, resentment vs Multiplicity.
- *Dedicated Reactionary*: Rightness, hate of Otherness, no overt anxiety. Has all answers for Multiplicity.
- *Negativism*: Passive resistance vs Authority, but no cause of one's own.
- *Dogmatic Rebel*: Identity in 'cause' without contingent judgment. 'Cause' determined by whatever Authority does to be against.

It is not difficult to see people in these states in our society, even without a deeper understanding of Perry's work. And whichever way you look at it, it is easy to see these 'retreat' pathways leading to falling in with gang culture, or to fundamentalist beliefs, which in their different ways provide strongly reinforced and unilateral values, with dogmatic answers to any questions that may arise. Questions would, of course, be strongly discouraged.

Just as personal development planning only makes sense when people begin to conceive of themselves as able to achieve, so ethical development only makes sense when people are ready to contemplate – or to hold in mind as plausible – different possible personal values. Before that time, young or immature people need to be in a more secure environment – one that will help them grow and develop until they are ready to deal positively with pluralism.

Holding in mind different possible values is not the same as unreflectively acting on different sets of values in different contexts. People's lives may well span different contexts that demand different values, but they may simply never reflect on the conflict between the values in those different contexts. Perhaps it is even the norm for young people to go through a stage like this, where they act according to different values in different situations, but do not reflect. As discussed previously, this may be associated with acute embarrassment when behaviour suitable to one context is revealed in another context.

We could see the related stage of ethical development as involving the recognition and development of personalities and values. It is founded on the experience of care, warmth, love and security, which provide the basis on which a young person starts to acknowledge different authorities, different values, and then different contexts and different personalities. I cannot think of a better popular introduction to this more basic part of human development than the book, *Families and How to Survive Them*, by Robin Skynner and John Cleese. Skynner, along with most family therapists, places a high value on a loving and stable family, which he sees as ideally having a father and a mother.

So how, in our society, can we maximise the chances that children have a loving and stable family? Perhaps, by motivating young people to understand and explore their values early on, when they are ready, but before having children of their own, so that they can partner with someone with similar core values, where there will be mutual respect and a greater chance of long-term satisfaction, and thus stability.

I'll finish this section with two groups of questions that it would be useful to answer, to be able to take ethical development forward in practice. These questions do, however, raise many issues unrelated to e-portfolios, so I will not attempt to answer the questions, and will rather leave them open for you to consider.

Is there a place, and if so, what, for religion in ethical development? Religious organisations are usually involved in some way with questions of how people should live, and their (moral) values, but it is clear that many people see religious approaches (other than their own, if they have one) as undermining the values in society that they hold as important. How can we distinguish between helpful and unhelpful religion? Is any kind of religious fundamentalism compatible with the relativism, in Perry's sense, that is a vital later stage of personal ethical development, or with a recognition that different values are appropriate in different contexts? Can the absolute answers of fundamentalist approaches give the security that some people need, at least temporarily, as a step on the way?

Should schools and other educational institutions have personal values and their development as part of the curriculum? Many schools at present make an attempt to stand for certain values, and to instil them in their pupils, by example, and through the processes that take place in the school. But to what extent is it feasible and desirable to go beyond this, to helping school pupils recognise and develop their own values, which would mean acknowledging that the values put forward by the school are not absolute? How do we recognise when a young person is ready for that next stage in ethical development? And should this be part of the personalisation of education?

The values associated with e-portfolio tools and practices

I believe that e-portfolio technology and practice is not intrinsically biased towards any particular view of life, but on the other hand, I don't think it is all entirely neutral. The associated values could be called 'meta-values', that is, they are values about values, rather than being the ordinary sort of values about behaviour that people normally discuss.

The fact that e-portfolio practice is so often closely linked to reflection and reflective practice suggests that reflection is one of these meta-values. Socrates seems to have shared this meta-value, and it is expressed in his saying: 'the unexamined life is not worth living'. Reflection includes the possibility of reflecting on values, with the possible consequence of growing towards coherence, consistency and commitment. Alternatively, to repeat my earlier phrase, 'personal integrity reflection across contexts' is something that could lead to good, both for the individual and for society.

The fact that e-portfolios are (normally) presentations arranged by the portfolio holder implies valuing your ability and freedom to define yourself, rather than being defined by others. Of course, you may choose to accept a definition of yourself given by someone else – but if you accept it after reflection, you would have taken it on as your own.

The fact of e-portfolios providing evidence for abilities and achievements implies valuing your abilities and achievements, alongside the achievements of everyone else, each valued in the terms of the person who achieved it.

The fact that e-portfolio tools help you to organise information about yourself implies valuing being able to control the information about yourself, rather than not knowing about it, or leaving it in the hands of others.

The fact that e-portfolio tools normally allow you to organise information in your own way implies valuing your own organisation schemes for your own information, rather than making you organise your own information in someone else's terms.

To be useful to other people, information from e-portfolios needs to be reasonably reliable. This implies valuing honesty and holding a negative view regarding any wilful misrepresentation. As is the case with CVs, many people recognise this as a potential weak point. As well as technical solutions, maybe we need, as a society, to build up values and related practices that lead to the reliability of portfolio information.

To value diversity would also help with reliability. The more diverse ways there are to succeed, and the more you are able to find an individual way suited to yourself – to succeed in your own terms – the less there is any incentive to pretend to be something that you are not.

Trustworthiness, as a value, needs attention, because if it were not present in society, and if, as a result, e-portfolios became simply works of fiction, depicting how people think they might come across best, it would destroy their usefulness for any kind of automatic matching or selection.

Another idea that could conceivably improve the reliability of value claims would be a culture that supports the playful tentative exploration of values. If people's (non-harmful) imagined desires can be acted out safely to their satisfaction, there might be that much less temptation to mix fantasy with reality in the portfolios one presents for real-world purposes. But then, what is imaginary and what is real? As with double lives, often all that is needed to play a role successfully is to be able to keep it up consistently for a few hours at a time. If you have evidence that you can do that, why should you not play that role in real life some of the time, as you are able and willing?

References and further reading

For Circles of Support and Accountability, see the Circles UK website (*http://www.circles-uk.org.uk/*).

After drafting this chapter, I recently came across Peter Block's *Community: the Structure of Belonging* (2008), which gives much detail about how to set up small groups in communities, geared towards change.

Two books previously mentioned in previous chapters are William G. Perry's *Forms of Intellectual and Ethical Development in the College Years: A Scheme* (1970, 1999) and Robin Skynner and John Cleese's *Families and How to Survive Them* (1983).

25

The culture of information and choice: an analogy with the development of agriculture

I have no specialist knowledge of ancient history and prehistory. I probably share my vague ideas about what happened at the dawn of civilisation with many other people, and that is just as well: the points I make in this chapter are not speculations about the actual development of agriculture, but rather analogies with commonsense ideas about the development of civilisation that could throw light on a turning point in our present time.

I imagine a prehistory where people lived in small groups of hunter-gatherers. (If nothing else, then the small size is supported by the work of Robin Dunbar, whose upper limit for the size of early human social groups – around 150 – has come to be called 'Dunbar's number'.) When food was obtained, most of it would be eaten – a pattern that can be seen in many wild animals. Some of it would be cooked, and some, if it stored well, perhaps stored for a while. But mainly, food would be found because people were hungry, or could imagine being hungry soon. The response to people being hungry, or envisaging hunger soon, would be to go and find more food – quite a direct connection.

This cannot be done directly when there are larger groups of people coming together in towns and cities. Wild food growing nearby would soon all be eaten; wild animals hunted for food would be killed off, or retreat further away from the city; local fish stocks would run out. Thus, towns and cities – civilisation – needed to await a more organised approach to food supply, namely, agriculture.

One might imagine some early hunter-gatherers talking about these new-fangled ideas about agriculture. Agriculture could have seemed hopelessly implausible. Who could possibly be expected to organise society in such a structured way, so that crops were sown, tended, harvested and stored away in an annual cycle that had nothing to do with the rhythms of people's hunger? Wasn't it just far too much to ask of people? Who on earth would do that unless there was some extremely strong motivation to do so? Even for animal husbandry, could you expect people to spend all that time looking after animals instead of just simply hunting them and eating them?

But despite what may have looked like great implausibility, agriculture actually happened, and the whole relationship between humanity and food changed, becoming more regulated. Instead of being driven by hunger to find more food, an incredible amount of human organisation was established. As well as enabling quite different forms of human culture, this required large changes in the way people behaved, and we can imagine that we still have traces of those changes, and the resulting organisation of society, in today's culture.

How does my simplistic view of the origin of human agriculture relate to information? As far as I can make out, for all of history up to and largely including the present, we have generally been living with a hunter-gatherer approach to information. Is this the best way to continue in the future? Is it even sustainable in the long term? It may rather be that a change in our approach to dealing with information, just like the change in our approach to dealing with food in the transition from hunting and gathering to agriculture, could open up new possibilities for civilisation, even though the changes may look as implausible at present as I imagine agriculture looked to the average hunter-gatherer.

As an illustration of our hunter-gatherer approach to information, let's take the examples we have mentioned before, of employment and jobs, and friendship and friends.

Many people – I imagine the majority – go about job-seeking in something like the following way. While I am suitably and stably occupied, in a job or other occupation, I take little notice of other employment opportunities. It is only as the end of a period of occupation approaches, or if I am in some way dissatisfied with my current job, that I start to consider what I might like to do next. At that point, I might try to assemble a fair amount of information about employment opportunities, and when an opportunity looks inviting, I might look again at my CV, and rewrite it for the particular opportunity that appeals to me. That process of rewriting is quite detailed, because I have to work out what the employers are looking for, and then reflect on my past experiences to think what I might present as evidence to demonstrate what they are looking for. The 'hunter-gatherer' style of this approach is apparent in the way in which I gather and process most of the information near to the time of use. But because the processes are quite time-consuming, and time presses, I am likely to settle for a job that is 'good enough', rather than one which would be truly well suited to me.

How do we find and make friends? I don't know of anyone taking a particularly planned approach to that. What seems usual is for us to be sociable, join clubs and social networks, initiate and respond to conversations in whatever settings we find ourselves with other people. If there seems to be a spark of mutual interest, then we follow it. But most of the people with whom we interact socially remain either anonymous or just acquaintances. I don't think many people keep dossiers full of the details of potential friends (though many do subscribe to internet dating services). Perhaps it is as well that making friends has a certain randomness about it, but it does mean that we are less likely to meet the people with whom we could be really close friends.

What does the analogy suggest about how finding employment and friends might be done differently?

We can imagine a hunter-gatherer asking, 'how can we live in bigger groups?' This raises questions like 'can a group of such size last a winter without going out hunting?' to which the answer would be clearly 'no!' until someone had figured out effective food storage systems. In fact, without effective food storage systems, agriculture would be largely pointless. Once humans discovered both ways of transporting and storing food, and ways of producing food that could be transported and stored, it became possible both to produce food far away, and to survive the changing seasons. It became possible to experiment in urban living, and to discover its possibilities.

Perhaps the analogy is becoming more clear. Once we start being able to store information in such a way that it is accessible when needed – information related to ourselves certainly, but also information about other people, about organisations, and about things – this opens up possibilities for changing our hunter-gatherer ways with information. Instead of ending up with jobs that are just 'good enough' to keep up with common expectations, it might become realistic for us to look for jobs that are really very well suited to us. Employers might start to expect employees that are really well-suited to the job, and happy in it, and they might start to find those employees without the vast expenditure of time or money that currently plagues recruitment, and, even more so, executive search, or 'head-hunting'.

On the social front, with the popularisation of the web, people now join business and social networks in which it is possible to store information about ourselves, in a way that helps us to find others, and others to find us, when appropriate. And these networks do store a lot of information. But we still lack good methods of finding people who are really appropriate to our present needs, even with those networks in place. As suggested above, one cause of this is that people don't know what they really need, because they don't know enough about their own values, and because they don't understand how values, personality and their contexts work. Put another way, closer to the analogy, I could say that they haven't stored any reliable and machine-processable information about their values, because they haven't got any. We haven't grown those crops yet, and the storehouses have not been fitted out to receive that particular crop.

To reap the full benefit of the harvest of information about ourselves and our values, we have to store that information in ways that are machine-processable. The industrial revolution took thousands of years to come after the (first, Neolithic) agricultural revolution, finally to give a rich selection of ways to store food. But for the storage of information, all the necessary information revolution has already happened. The technology is there, and it is our understanding that is lagging behind.

When we do find reliable ways of growing personal values, and harvesting machine-processable information about them, it will surely have the potential to transform society. That transformation, I believe, will be no lesser than the transformation enabled by agriculture. Theodore Zeldin's vision of 'What becomes possible when soul-mates meet' is an inspiring image of the potential of people meeting, when their values are close, and who complement each other in ability, or quality, or whatever is practically necessary. The meetings recounted by Zeldin are exceptional. But with the technology, why should not many more soul-mates meet? Even if many met at this level, we could hardly call this kind of meeting 'common', as to those meeting it would still be marvellous. But if, in our modern world, there is the prospect of the majority of humanity becoming affluent, why should the majority of humanity not also enjoy these remarkable meetings? Could not the majority of work be based on the outcome of those meetings, with people working together in ethically-sound common causes, leading to their fulfilment, and to the world's benefit?

Another writer I have found inspiring, Ricardo Semler, supplies another piece of the jigsaw of putting together satisfying work. In his books, such as *Maverick*, he describes aspects of his highly successful company culture. One thing that happens in his company is that units are restricted in size to around Dunbar's number, and if one grows too much beyond this number, it is required to split up. Another very surprising feature of his business is that the working culture is extremely transparent – people know exactly what everyone else does and earns. This transparency is helped by limiting the size of the unit as described. But then, within that culture of transparency, there is a very surprising amount of autonomy and choice for each individual, bounded by the limit that if you are not valued by your colleagues, they won't renew your contract.

Agriculture made towns and cities possible, made it possible to meet and associate with far more people than was possible in hunter-gatherer tribes. Eventually, poets could meet poets, artists could meet artists, and musicians, musicians. The potential of a group of competent musicians is so much greater than the sum of them all in ones and twos. But large cities have been with us for thousands of years now, and somehow the advances brought on by civilisation seem to have run dry, and urban decay has begun to manifest. Provided that people can still communicate and work together, the next step forward in human cultural terms might well be independent from physical proximity – it might be through association by choice.

Perhaps now is a good time for the better application of those information technologies that have been developed in recent decades, in supporting storage and reuse: not of food, as in neolithic times, nor even of money, where information technology applied to finance has enabled both wonderful and dreadful things. It is now the turn of personal information to be the focus of the new technology – information technology – so that we can present ourselves and the values we have chosen to others, and let that information be used for the further positive transformation of society. I hope this book has given a clearer insight into one possible way of working towards that good goal.

References and further reading

Robin Dunbar (1997) *Grooming, Gossip and the Evolution of Language.*
Theodore Zeldin (1995) *An Intimate History of Humanity.*
Ricardo Semler (1993) *Maverick.*

26

In conclusion?

I'm sure you care about other people: no doubt you care about many of those you know; probably you also care about people you don't know. But just focusing on the people you know, for a moment, how many of them are in situations that are less than ideal for them? If your experience is anything like mine, I'd guess there are plenty. And for those friends, it's not mainly about material possessions, is it? On reflection, isn't it more likely to be that they have a job that doesn't suit them, or they have no job, perhaps because they have not found something that they find fulfilling? Or perhaps, they have the wrong friends, or are mixed up with the wrong people. Or perhaps they do not have a suitable life partner. Or maybe their job is OK, their partner is OK, but they just need to meet the right people, to get an opportunity that really makes a difference to their lives. Or maybe they just need to find their own purpose in life, and their own values.

So, I naturally invite you to reflect on what I have written in this book. What would happen if these people you know were to explore and discover their own values, and were able to get together with more people who shared those values, to live and work in ways that really suited them? How would that change their lives? What if the technology existed, and was easily accessible, to enable them to explore and develop their values, and use that information to their advantage, and to the advantage of others?

And what about society – your own society, and societies in other parts of the world? Can you envisage society changing if this kind of personal development, including development of personal values, were to become common; perhaps if society looked more like the kind of e-portfolio social environment sketched out in Chapter 20?

And I'd like to tie this conclusion back to the introduction, in Chapter 1, where I asked who you are, O reader. Now I ask who you might be, and who you might become, O reader. If you were to explore these questions in the company of people, even just one or two, who you really trust, because their values are close enough to yours, where could those questions lead you?

And how long might all this take? Even for each one of us individually, and certainly for society as a whole, I see it as a long journey. But I think it is worth setting off in the right direction now, because we already have some of the tools that are needed, and we have the technology to develop the rest. If your values are close enough to mine, how about us joining each other on this journey? I would hope our efforts can work together positively, towards building the tools, researching and trying out the methods, and publicising the results.

Are conclusions meant to be answers? Or are genuine conclusions, on things that matter, really just new sets of questions?

Glossary: Terminology, notes and abbreviations

The chapters where each term is used, more than in passing, are given, and chapters where the concept is discussed or used more deeply are given in **bold italics**. References to other terms listed here are given *italics*, while definitions drawn from other sources are, depending on their length, given either in quotes or as indented quotes.

ability, competence, competency, knowledge, skill

See: Chapters 3, 5, 6, 8, 11, 14, 21

This range of related concepts concerns what people know about, know how to do, or can do. Some writers make the distinction between competence, as taking into account the context, and competency, as being context-free. Other distinctions are also sometimes made. However, the practical value of these distinctions can be questioned, as people set out and define what they require or what they claim to have, often without reference to these distinctions. At best, the distinctions may help people to think about the topics.

achievement

See: Chapters 6, 9

This describes a state of the world that has been brought about at least partly by the agency of the *portfolio holder*. To be worth putting in a *portfolio*, the portfolio holder must believe that it is positive evidence of something desirable in the audience's eyes.

action plan, action planning

See: Chapters 5, 9

An action plan is a considered plan to achieve one or more of the *portfolio holder*'s goals or purposes; action planning is normally understood as some kind of systematic planning for the future, often understood to be part of general *PDP* processes, and possibly involving some kind of experiential learning cycle including the creation of action plans. E-portfolio tools can be, and often are, used to support action planning, and for the recording of action plans, by helping the *portfolio holder* to structure the plan and the planning process.

activity, experience

See: Chapters 6, 8

This refers to any activity, experience or occupation that takes any time and involves the *portfolio holder* in any way: future, present or past, continuous, interrupted or recurrent; it can comprise a group of lesser activities.

A meeting is a kind of activity.

assessment

See: Chapters 2, 5, 6, 8, 9, 10, *11*, 20

I won't try to define assessment, as it is reasonably well understood. Rather, I will just point out, first, that assessment can be either 'formative' or 'summative' (or both together), that is, either directed generally towards shaping further learning, or towards taking stock of a current state, whether or not that state is the result of learning. Second, some kind of assessment is essential to the whole concept of a *portfolio*, because a *portfolio* presents *personal information* to some audience, and the *portfolio holder* wants the audience to assess something about the holder or their work in a certain way. *Reflection* might also be seen, very generally, as a form of self-assessment.

context (in the sense of type, or kind, of situation)

See: Chapter 22

A set of situations, as seen from the perspective of an individual, in which that person tends to behave with consistent, coherent *personal values*. In each context which is taken as different, an individual may adopt a characteristic *personality*, involving various aspects of self-presentation. These contexts tend to be held separate due to their different requirements for self-presentation.

continuing professional development (CPD)

See: Chapter 6

critical friend

See: Chapter 23

This is a convenient label for the kind of close friend who knows you in more than one *context*, and is therefore in a good position to help you reflect across *contexts*, to promote your *ethical development*. My sense is that this idea fits well with the other uses of the term. Wikipedia currently provides this definition:

> A critical friend can be defined as a trusted person who asks provocative questions, provides data to be examined through another lens, and offers critiques of a person's work as a friend. A critical friend takes the time to fully understand the context of the work presented and the outcomes that the person or group is working toward. The friend is an advocate for the success of that work.

curriculum vitae (CV), résumé

See: Chapters 2, 4, 6, 9, *20*

One of the interesting things about the concept of a CV is how it has changed, and continues to change, to reflect what people take as significant to present to others. However, it is difficult to stretch the concept of a CV to embrace a rich *e-portfolio*, with all its linked evidence and *reflection*. Perhaps we can see the *e-portfolio* as a natural successor to the CV. In the terms of Chapter 20, the CV's place is in societies based on mass testing; the *e-portfolio* properly belongs in more advanced societies.

education

See: Chapters 8, *10*

I would hesitate to offer my own definition of education, as it would add little to anyone's understanding. However, an *ISO* working group (ISO SC36_WG2_N0012) has defined education thus:

> activities which aim at developing the knowledge, skills, moral values and understanding required in all aspects of life rather than a knowledge and skill relating to only a limited field of activity. The purpose of education is to provide the conditions essential to young people and adults to develop an understanding of the traditions and ideas influencing the society in which they live and to enable them to make a contribution to it. It involves the study of their own cultures and the laws of nature, as well as the acquisition of linguistic and other skills which are basic to learning, personal development, creativity and communication.

e-learning

See: Chapters 2, 3, 10, 14, 16

Learning which takes place through exchange between a combination of learning resources, tasks and support systems (human or otherwise) where the exchange is mediated through *ICT*.

e-portfolio

Used throughout

An e-portfolio is a *portfolio* in which the information is collected, held and displayed electronically, that is, with the use of *ICT*. If the distinction between e-portfolio and *portfolio* is not important somewhere, often the term *portfolio* by itself is used instead, with the intention of including the meaning of e-portfolio.

employee development

See: Chapters 5, 14, *15*

Employee development encompasses processes that take into account the needs both of *employers* and employees, which may include aspects both of more traditional skills training and staff development, and of the more individual-oriented or holistic *PDP* and *CPD*.

employers and employment

See: Chapters 2, 3, 5–8, 11, 14, 15, 19, *21*, 23–25

I would add nothing to people's understanding by trying to define employment. The significant thing about employment, from the perspective of *e-portfolios*, is that employers want competent people, and people can claim and demonstrate their competences through *e-portfolios*.

ethical development

See: Chapters *23, 24*

Ethical development is the process by which an individual comes to recognise the values they hold and express in different *contexts*, to compare and contrast those values, and to change the values expressed in one or more *contexts*. This also includes the process of reclassifying situations into *contexts*, so that either the boundaries of some *contexts* shift, or one *context* is split into more than one, or previously different *contexts* are brought into one.

I also intend the term to imply the development of *personal values* in the light of ethics, and the values of society, more widely.

Ethical development is not ethical, in this sense, in virtue of it promoting any particular set of 'good' or approved values, but rather in promoting the development of *personal values*, which in my view counts as a good thing.

information and communication technology (ICT)

See: Chapters 6, 8, 17

This includes computer and telephony equipment, and the networks that are used in communications between them. The term generally extends to include both the information systems that use that technology, and the common services delivered through the technology.

identity

See: Chapters 22, 23

This term has been used in many ways. This book does not focus on the term, but uses it generally to refer to the subjective sense associated with a particular *personality* and set of related values.

interoperability

See: Chapters 7, 16, 17, *18*, 19

In *e-portfolio* discussions, interoperability generally refers to whether two or more systems can work in compatible ways with the same information. At least two aspects can be distinguished, the first of which is the technical portability of information between the systems: this aspect of interoperability is present if each system can export information in a form that can be imported by the others, and requires a suitable and effective interoperability specification to use as the format for transferring the information.

Building on this, information with the same meaning in different systems can be represented by those systems in the same way. This suggests that different systems can use the same information to perform similar functions for similar purposes, even if two different systems cover different functions and therefore cannot be directly substituted. This could be called 'semantic' interoperability.

Because it is natural for portfolio-related tools to offer different functionality, this book focuses mostly on the first aspect. But there is little or no point in transferring information between systems where the processes producing the information in the first system are incompatible with the processes which might use the information in the second system.

ISO

The International Organization for Standardization, or one of its standards.

learner

Used throughout.

Glossary

On the grounds that all people learn in some sense at all times, a learner can be any individual person, but especially, any person consciously and voluntarily engaged in learning or the management of their own learning.

Liverpool University Student Interactive Database (LUSID)

See: Chapters 8, 23

LUSID is a web-based tool devised in 1997 to help students record their experiences, analyse the employability skills used in those experiences, carry out self-audits of the skills, find resources for self-study development, and perhaps do *action planning* and construct skills-oriented *CVs*.

metadata

See: Chapter 6

The term is mentioned rather than used in this book, because of disagreements about its meaning. Strictly, it should be data about data: thus, information such as author, date of creation, etc. about a record in a system; but just as metadata about a book can be very extensive, the term is often understood more broadly to mean just about any information about something apart from its actual information content.

NVQ

See: Chapter 11

National Vocational Qualifications (in England and Wales), or Scottish Vocational Qualifications in Scotland, are work-related, competence-based qualifications. Further information is available from a number of web pages, presently including:

- *http://www.direct.gov.uk/en/EducationAndLearning/Qualifications Explained/DG_10039029*
- *http://en.wikipedia.org/wiki/National_Vocational_Qualification*
- *http://www.qca.org.uk/qca_6640.aspx*

personal development planning (PDP)

See: Chapters 5–7, 10, 13, 14, 21, Appendix

It is difficult to better the widely-quoted definition held by the UK Quality Assurance Agency for Higher Education:

> a structured and supported process undertaken by an individual to reflect on their learning, performance and/or achievement and to plan for their personal, educational and career development.

This definition is currently held on the QAA website (*http://www.qaa.ac.uk/ academicinfrastructure/progressfiles/archive/policystatement/default .asp#pdp*).

persona, personality

See: Chapters 6, 9, 12, 21, **22**, 23, 24

Rita Carter suggests this definition: 'a coherent and characteristic way of seeing, thinking, feeling and behaving'. In Part 3, I elaborate my view that each individual has a persona or personality associated with each *context* distinguished by that individual. In this view, the salient distinctions between personalities are the personal values held and expressed in the *context* where that personality is displayed, and this relates closely to behaviour, as in Carter's definition.

personal development

See: most chapters

Personal development encompasses *PDP*, but is a slightly broader concept. It also includes processes that are neither structured nor supported, but that in some way result in greater realisation of one's personal potential. Generally, personal development is motivated primarily by the interests of the individual, while staff development, in contrast, is motivated primarily by the interests of the employer. *Employee development* is the attempt to reconcile these interests, while *ethical development* is a kind of personal development.

personal information

See: Chapters *3*, *4*, 6, 7, *12*, 13, 16, *21*, 23, 25

Personal information is a term used in data protection acts in the UK, and no doubt similar terms are used elsewhere. In this book, I use the term to mean any information related to a person, either about that person, or in which the person is identified, e.g. as author. It is not necessarily 'owned' by the person, and in any case ownership is a tricky concept with respect to information. Just about any personal information could be stored, in one or other form, in an e-*portfolio system*, and then become e-*portfolio information*. Most, but not necessarily all, information stored in an e-*portfolio system* will be personal information in this sense.

personal values

Used throughout Part 3

Personal values represent the inner dispositions of an individual to choose certain possible actions or inaction (including speech) over other possible actions. These may be related to consciously-held values, such as moral principles, in which case the choice may be deliberate. However, I consider such patterns of consistently choosing one behaviour over another to represent personal values, whether or not the values are consciously held, or the actions are taken deliberately. One possible indicator of values being discussed in English is the use of the word 'should'.

portfolio

Used throughout

As current thinking about portfolios is developing, definitions are still being proposed and discussed. A relatively simple definition, in line with many others, and which suits this book, is that a portfolio is a purposeful selection of items and information for presentation to a deliberately chosen audience. This is to be distinguished from a *portfolio tool* or *portfolio system*. A portfolio may be electronically held and presented, as an *e-portfolio*, or it may be based on older technologies.

portfolio holder

See: Chapters 1, 4, 6, 13, 16, 18

The portfolio holder is the person to whom the information in a *portfolio* relates. This person would normally be expected to use some *portfolio system* to manage the information and produce *portfolios*. Portfolio holders who are children, or otherwise not fully responsible, may have other people to help in these tasks, or to do them on their behalf. The portfolio holder, in this sense, is not to be confused with the institution or organisation providing the *portfolio system*, along with the storage of information. Such an organisation may hold the data, but it does not hold the *portfolios*.

portfolio system, portfolio tool

Used interchangeably and throughout.

A portfolio system is any system or tool that helps a *portfolio holder* to collect and manage *portfolio information*, and either to reflect on that information, possibly in the process adding to it, or from that information to select and present *portfolios* to chosen audiences. Portfolio tools often are designed to help with *PDP* and other related processes.

portfolio information

See: Chapters 1, 3, 5, 6, 7, 8

Any set of *portfolio item*s, together with information about relationships between those items and between the items and external resources.

portfolio item

See: Chapters 6, 9, 18

A portfolio item is a self-contained unit of information which can be used by the *portfolio holder* as a whole in any chosen setting. This does not include the relationships between portfolio items. Commonly recognised types of portfolio item include *ability, achievement, action plan* and *activity*; other kinds include the types of *personal information* that may occur in *CVs* or be used for *PDP*.

privacy

See: Chapters 1, 4, 13–15

Because e-*portfolio tools* exist in part to present information to other people, an important aspect of privacy is that viewing permissions can be effectively controlled by the *portfolio holder*, and that access to the holder's *personal information* without proper authorisation by the holder is prevented. However, just as in the traditional world, once information is given to anyone, it is no longer safe in any case, and may find its way to people for whom it was not intended.

reflection

See: most chapters

Reflection could be simply defined as the bringing to mind of some past experience or event, with the intention or the result of learning something from it. This contrasts with a mere reminiscence, which people can do again and again without learning anything new. Reflection is connected deeply with *portfolio*s, as a *portfolio* can act as the record of the experience or event, and can act both as a prompt for reflection, and as a factor towards the accuracy of later recollection.

security

See: Chapters 7, 11, 15, 16

The primary sense in which the term is used is about how secure e-*portfolio information* is from unauthorised access from other people. Secondarily (chapters not listed) it refers to how secure people are psychologically, as a precondition of *ethical development.*

Semantic Web

See: Chapters 7, 19

On the homepage for the Semantic Web (*http://www.w3.org/2001/sw/*), the World Wide Web Consortium (W3C) uses the following definition, which, by itself, is not very informative:

The Semantic Web provides a common framework that allows data to be shared and reused across application, enterprise, and community boundaries. It is a collaborative effort led by W3C with participation from a large number of researchers and industrial partners.

The significance of the Semantic Web to this book is that *portfolio information* can readily be represented in a basic form which is congruent with Semantic Web structures. This is a 'graph' (i.e. a diagram) with nodes, drawn perhaps as blobs, each representing a single *portfolio item*, with arrows joining them, representing the relationships between the items.

uniform resource identifier (URI)

See: Chapters 8, 19

uniform resource locator (URL)

See: Chapters 8, 19

Appendix:
Personal development planning

These lists were assembled over a period in 2002 and 2003 when Helen Richardson and I were surveying current personal development planning (PDP) practice in the UK. The practice was mainly paper-based, but there was a considerable coherence between what was done in different institutions, across schools, colleges and universities. The list of activities was essentially taken directly from what was happening, while the list of information types was slightly extrapolated to cover what we thought might be relevant, as well as what we directly identified on forms.

List of PDP activities

1. Discussing learner's personal situation/experiences
2. Compiling list of experiences or past activities, including employment
3. Reviewing and reflecting on logs
4. Reviewing past written goals and action plans against more recent experience
5. Reviewing experience in response to guidance
6. Reviewing coursework performance and course experience
7. Reviewing critical incidents
8. Listing achievements/qualifications (with documentation if available)
9. Relating experiences to skills (or vice versa)
10. Reviewing/profiling/auditing skills
11. Reviewing progress in/development of skills
12. Reviewing personal interests
13. Reviewing/reflecting on personal attitudes/values

14 Assembling evidence for skills
15 Assessing own learning style
16 Setting goals for skills development
17 Setting goals related to subject development
18 Setting more general personal/social goals
19 Relating goals to motivations and reasons
20 Originating CV/personal statement/other compilation
21 Revising CV/personal statement/other compilation
22 Originating action plan for the achievement of academic goals
23 Revising action plan for academic goals in the context of feedback/discussion
24 Originating action plan for personal goals/skills development
25 Revising action plan for personal goals in the context of feedback/discussion
26 Doing exercises alone for skill development
27 Participating in workshops/classes/sessions for skills development
28 Choosing/evaluating suitability of course/module/employment/position
29 Writing application for position/employment/course/programme
30 Writing log (for learning or reflection)
31 Writing individual learning plan
32 Negotiating learning/employment contract

List of PDP information types

1 Statement of learner's personal situation
2 Statement/list of past activities/experiences/employment
3 Reflective writing, referring either to experiences or to journals/logs
4 Statement of learning from experience
5 Statement of performance on task or goal
6 Statement/list of formal qualifications
7 Statement/list of other achievements
8 Statement/list of skills

Appendix

9 Evaluation of skills on a scale
10 Identified strengths and weaknesses in skills
11 Evidence for skills
12 Statement/list of personal interests
13 Statement of learner's attitudes/values
14 Statement of learning preferences
15 Statement of reasons for present module/programme/position
16 Statement of current goals without stated motivation
17 Statement of current goals with stated motivation
18 Statement of motivation/aspirations for future position/employment/course
19 CV/personal statement/other compilation of above items
20 Action plan where learner is not directed to particular type of goal
21 Action plan towards next life stage (position, employment or study)
22 Action plan for skills development
23 Action plan for academic /educational/work-related goal(s)
24 Action plan for personal/social goal(s)
25 Learning log or journal intended for later reflection
26 Statement of learner support provided (past) or required (future)
27 Statement of other resources available or required
28 Learning/employment contract (include mention of skills)
29 Individual learning plan
30 Learner's identification and contact details
31 Learner's affiliation, membership etc.
32 Tutor's identification and contact details
33 Tutor's membership of and role in the institution
34 Learner's current enrolment in educational programmes, modules etc.
35 Official relationships
36 Other staff member's details, e.g. administrator
37 Other staff member's role, etc.
38 About an institution or body
39 Programmes, modules, activities, employment proposed or on offer

40 Framework of skill definitions
41 Information or training material on PDP-related skills
42 Date, location, attendance at event/meeting appointment
43 Timetable for learner's future scheduled activities
44 History of the user's actions in/interaction with a PDP system
45 User's preferences, needs or requirements concerning IT system use
46 IT system navigation and search
47 Corporate validation of a document or of records
48 A tutor's validation of a document or of records
49 A learner's validation of a document or of records

Bibliography

In case anyone has a use for academic-style references, or just for interest, here are the references to works published as books, collected from the chapter references. Of course, many works, particularly popular ones, are published in various editions by several publishers, possibly at different dates. But at least the ISBNs given here represent one published edition – the one I own in cases where I do own a copy of the book. ISBNs can also be searched for, to find an edition on the web rather more quickly than through author or title, and I have given them without spaces or hyphens, which is the easiest form to use. I have a preference for giving the year of original publication and copyright, even when the version with that ISBN may have been published later.

Aalderink, W. and Veugelers, M. (eds) (2007) *Stimulating Lifelong Learning: The E-portfolio in Dutch Higher Education.* Utrecht: SURF. ISBN: 9789078887072.

Baume, D. (2003) *Supporting Portfolio Development.* York: Learning and Teaching Support Network Generic Centre. ISBN: 1904190359.

Block, P. (2008) *Community: The Structure of Belonging.* San Francisco, CA: Berrett-Koehler Publishers. ISBN: 9781576754870.

Cambridge, B.L., Kahn, S., Tompkins, D. P. and Yancey, K. B. (eds) (2001) *Electronic Portfolios: Emerging Practices in Student, Faculty and Institutional Learning.* Washington, DC: American Association for Higher Education. ISBN: 1563770504.

Cambridge, D., Cambridge, B. and Yancey, K. B. (2008) *Electronic Portfolios 2.0: Emergent Research on Implementation and Impact,* Sterling, VA: Stylus. ISBN: 9781579223212.

Carter, R. (2008) Multiplicity: *The New Science of Personality.* London: Little, Brown. ISBN: 9780316730884.

Checkland, P. (1981) *Systems Thinking, Systems Practice.* Chichester: John Wiley. ISBN: 0471279110.

Dunbar, R. (1996) *Grooming, Gossip and the Evolution of Language.* Cambridge, MA: Harvard University Press. ISBN: 0674363361.

Goffman, E. (1959) *The Presentation of Self in Everyday Life.* London, Penguin. ISBN: 0140135715.

Hall, B., Kalven, J., Rosen, L., and Taylor, B. (1991) *Developing Human Values.* Fond du Lac, WI: International Values Institute of Marian College. ISBN: 1879494019.

Hallam, G. (project leader) et al. (2008) Australian ePortfolio Project, Queensland University of Technology. ISBN: 9781741072563.

Henderson, M. (2003) *Finding True North.* Auckland: HarperBusiness. ISBN: 1869504720.

Jourard, S. (1971) *The Transparent Self.* New York: Van Nostrand Reinhold. ISBN: 0442241925.

Kelly, G. (1955) *The Psychology of Personal Constructs.* New York: Norton. ISBN: 0415037999.

Kolb, D. (1984) *Experiential Learning: Experience as the Source of Learning and Development.* Upper Saddle River, NJ: Prentice-Hall. ISBN: 9780132952613.

Leitch, A. and HM Treasury (2006) *Leitch Review of Skills: Prosperity for All in the Global Economy – World Class Skills.* London: Stationery Office. ISBN: 9780118404860.

Mumford, E. (1983) *Designing Human Systems for New Technology: The ETHICS Method.* Manchester: Manchester Business School. ISBN: 0903808285.

Perry, W. G. (1968, 1999) *Forms of Intellectual and Ethical Development in the College Years: A Scheme.* San Francisco, CA: Jossey-Bass. ISBN: 0787941182.

Semler, R. (1993) *Maverick!* London: Arrow. ISBN: 9780099329411.

Skynner, R. and Cleese, J. (1983) *Families and How to Survive Them.* London: Vermilion. ISBN: 0749314109.

Windley, P. J. (2005) *Digital Identity.* Sebastopol, CA: O'Reilly. ISBN: 9780596008789.

Zeldin, T. (1994) *An Intimate History of Humanity.* London: Minerva. ISBN: 0749396237.

Index

abilities, 52–3, 221
accessibility, 102, 141
achievement, 221
  and goals, 50–2
action plan, 51, 53–4, 222
activities and experiences, 52, 222
administrative tools, 143–7
artefacts and other resources, 48
artistic talent, assessment of, 96
assertions, 50
assessment, 9–10, 84, 95, 222
  for learning, 29, 98
  management systems, 99
  of learning, 29, 98
  process, 100
  tools, 95
  and presentation, social environments of, 167–8
assessment centres, 96
asynchronous recording, 77
authentication, 58–60

blog entry, 45
blogging tools, 115
business networking systems, 114

circles of support and accountability, 206
claims, 50
co-counselling, 205
commercial source, 93–4

competency, 221
concepts, 44
context, 222
continuing professional development (CPD), 50–1, 68, 223
critical friend, 223
curriculum vitae (CV), 28, 40–2, 51, 53–4, 67, 80, 86, 169, 211, 214, 223

data protection outline, 57–8
decision-maker, 2
demotivation, 128
diagnostic assessments, 10
digital resources, 49
dualism, 191–2
Dublin Core, 55, 161
Dunbar's number, 213, 216

education, 224
educators, 17–18
e-learning, 224
  materials, 17
  system, 138
electronic non-portfolio options, 114–16
emotions, 197
employability, 85
  skills, 67
employee development, 31–3, 224
employers, 18–19, 31, 68, 215, 225

e-portfolio systems, principles of, 7–89
e-portfolio tools, 29, 85, 91–4, 101, 116, 200
　development of, 135–42
　use of, 157–64
e-portfolio, 47, 68, 224
　assessment strategy, 97–101
　information, 47–55
　principles, 83–9
　social environment, 170–1
　strategy, 145
　use, 9–14
　and employment, 225
ethical development, 203–12, 225
evidence, 54
　provision, 36
executive coaching, 32
extensional definitions, 44
extrinsic motivation, 127–8

folksonomy, 72
formative assessment, 29
free/open source, 93–4
freezing, 102
friends and the peer group, 20–1
functionality, 87–8

GNU General Public License, 147

Hall-Tonna, 201
Hall-Tonna Values Inventory, 172
high-stakes assessment, 95
historical practice, 39–41
HR-XML, 19, 62
human resources, 18

identity, 183–90, 226
IMS ePortfolio specification, 61
IMS LIP, 61
information interoperability, 60–3
information use/reuse, 24, 29–30

information and choice, culture of, 213–18
information and communication technology (ICT), 39, 225
　role of, 71–3
　strategy, 144
input and storage functions, 76–8
interoperability, 141–2, 149–56, 226
　specification, 146, 152
intrinsic motivation, 128
ISO, 226

job application, 13–14
Joint Information Systems Committee (JISC), 58
　CETIS, 62

key skills, 67
knowledge, 221

LEAP 2.0, 62
LEAP2A, 63
Learner Information Package (LIP), 61
learner, 2, 226
learning management system (LMS), 65
learning objectives, 84
learning processes, 84–5
life coaching, 32
life/work, 179
Liverpool University Student Interactive Database (LUSID), 68–9, 198, 227

maintenance, 78–81
management, 78–81
managing goals, 79
matching information, 175–82
matching process, 177
metadata, 227
meta-values, 210

Index

motivation, 33–4, 127–33
  reflection, 33–4
  goal setting, 33
  action planning, 33
  tool use of, 33–7
multiplicity, 208

National Occupational Standards, 69
  documentation, 71
National Vocational Qualifications (NVQs), 99, 169, 227
negativism, 208

open source software, 138

paper documentation, 59
PAPI Learner, 61
patterns and concepts, 52–3
patterns, 44
persona, 228
personal development planning (PDP), 34, 41, 50–1, 53, 60, 68, 84, 120, 123, 178, 228, 233–6
personal development, 31, 41, 85, 191–202, 228
  tools, 119–26
personal information management, 15–21, 23, 105, 225
  educators, 17–18
  employers, 18–19
  friends and peer group, 20–1
  of ourselves, 16–17
  public agencies, 19–20
  recording and storing, 23–5, 63–4
  recording information, 105–10
personal values, 183–202, 229
personality, 189–90, 228
phishing, 35
photographs, storage and management of, 16
plagiarism, 40

planning, 29
portfolio environments, 167–74
portfolio functionality, 75–82
portfolio holder, 48, 51, 79, 230
portfolio information, 39–73, 153–6, 230
  abilities, 52–3
  achievements and goals, 50–2
  action plans, 53–4
  activities and experience, 52
  artefacts and other resources, 48–9
  claims, 50
  common terms, 67
  CVs, 53–4
  evidence, 54
  expressions, 50
  issues, 57
  nature of, 43–5
  patterns and concepts, 52–3
  reflective writing, 50
  usage, 30–1
portfolio item, 230
portfolio purpose, 27–37
portfolio system, 230
portfolio tool, 230
  use of, 35–6
  related tools, 89
presentation, 10–11, 30
privacy, 231
problem-based learning approach, 12
professional development, 32, 40
public agencies, 19–20
public key infrastructure (PKI), 59
purposeful personal development, 29

recording information, 79
recording, act of, 16
records, 44–7
re-evaluation counselling, 205
reflection, 210, 231

reflective practitioner, 28
reflective purposes, 28–9
reflective writing, 40–2, 50
relativism, 208
reliable self-knowledge, 25
résumé, 40, 223
reuse and communication functions, 81–2
roles, 187–8

scientific management, 18
scrapbooks, 16
security, 102, 140, 231
self-presentation, 36, 111–17
Semantic Web, 157, 162, 231
Simple Knowledge Organization System (SKOS), 160
  mapping, 162
skills, development of, 11–12
social networking services, 114
Soft Systems Methodology, 131, 136
storage system, 109–10
student record system, 143
summative assessment, 30, 86, 102

tagging, practice of, 80
tools, 88–9
  for education, 88–9
Topic Maps, 157
transferable skills, 67

UK Data Protection Act, 57
UKLeaP, 61
uniform resource identifiers (URIs), 71, 157, 232
uniform resource locator (URL), 72, 92, 232
usability, 140–1

values, 188–9
  development of, 195–202
  tourism, 203–4
  and trust, 206–7
verification, 58–60
virtual learning environment (VLE), 9, 65

W3C's RDF primer, 162
work-life balance, 179
World Wide Web Consortium (W3C), 161